Founder Wealth Creation Through Equity Events

How Founders Build Personal Wealth Through Stock Ownership and Liquidity Events

By Joe Correa

Published by Live Stronger Faster

First Edition

Table of Contents

Introduction

The journey of building a company is often portrayed as a story about products, customers, innovation, and growth. Entrepreneurs are taught how to create businesses, raise capital, hire teams, generate revenue, and scale operations. Yet one of the most important subjects in entrepreneurship is often misunderstood, poorly planned, or completely ignored until it is too late: how founders actually create personal wealth through ownership.

Many business owners spend years building companies that generate revenue but fail to build lasting personal wealth because they never fully understand the power of equity events, ownership structures, liquidity planning, dilution management, and long-term capital strategy. A founder may create a successful company, attract millions in investment capital, generate strong revenue growth, and even achieve national recognition, yet still fail to convert that success into meaningful personal financial freedom. On the other hand, some founders build extraordinary wealth long before their companies become household names because they understand how ownership itself becomes one of the most valuable assets in the world. This book is about understanding that difference. Founder Wealth Creation Through Equity Events is designed to help entrepreneurs, startup founders, executives, investors, and business owners understand how wealth is truly created during the lifecycle of a growing company. This book explores the mechanisms that transform private ownership into life-changing financial opportunities. It explains how stock ownership, equity structures, liquidity events, acquisitions, secondary markets, IPOs, mergers, stock compensation, and capital markets all work together to create enormous wealth for founders who understand the system correctly.

In modern business, some of the largest fortunes in history have not been created through salaries. They were not built through hourly wages, consulting income, or even yearly business profits alone. The largest fortunes were built through ownership. Equity ownership became the engine that created billionaires, generational wealth, family offices, investment empires, and long-term financial freedom.

When founders create companies, they are not simply building products or services. They are building financial assets. Every customer acquired, every contract signed, every new market entered, every technology developed, and every strategic partnership established contributes to the value of the company itself. As valuation grows, ownership becomes increasingly valuable. This is the foundation of equity wealth creation. The power of founder equity is one of the most important concepts in the modern economy. A founder who owns a meaningful percentage of a company that eventually reaches a valuation of hundreds of millions or billions of dollars may generate more wealth from ownership appreciation than decades of traditional income could ever produce. This is why startup founders, technology entrepreneurs, SaaS creators, media company owners, and high-growth business operators often focus heavily on scaling enterprise value rather than maximizing short-term income.

Understanding equity changes how entrepreneurs think.

Instead of viewing a company purely as a source of monthly income, sophisticated founders begin viewing their business as a long-term wealth creation vehicle. They begin optimizing decisions around valuation growth, scalability, market positioning, recurring revenue, investor perception, and strategic expansion. They understand that every major business decision can affect future equity value and future liquidity opportunities.

This shift in thinking separates lifestyle businesses from scalable wealth-building companies.

One of the most misunderstood areas of founder wealth creation is dilution. Many entrepreneurs fear dilution because they believe giving away shares always weakens ownership.

While excessive dilution can absolutely reduce founder control and long-term wealth potential, strategic dilution can also become one of the most powerful tools for building larger enterprise value. A founder who owns 100% of a small company may be far less wealthy than a founder who owns 10% of a multi-billion-dollar company.

This concept is critical.

The goal is not necessarily to maintain maximum ownership at all costs. The goal is to maximize the long-term value of ownership. Strategic fundraising, institutional investment, venture capital, private equity partnerships, and public offerings can all dramatically increase enterprise value when used correctly. The challenge for founders is understanding when dilution creates leverage and when it creates unnecessary loss of control.

This book will explore how sophisticated founders think about ownership percentages, cap tables, fundraising rounds, stock option pools, investor negotiations, and long-term equity planning. Understanding these concepts can dramatically change the financial outcome of a founder's journey.

Another major focus of this book is liquidity events. Many entrepreneurs build valuable companies on paper but fail to create actual usable personal wealth because their ownership remains illiquid. A company may have a high valuation, but if there is no mechanism to convert ownership into cash, the founder may still face personal financial pressure despite operating a highly valuable business.

Liquidity events solve this problem.

A liquidity event occurs when ownership becomes convertible into cash or marketable assets. This may happen through an acquisition, merger, IPO, direct listing, secondary stock sale, recapitalization, buyout, or strategic investment transaction. These events often represent the moment when founders experience the financial rewards of years of work, sacrifice, risk, and execution.

Understanding liquidity strategy is essential because not all liquidity events are created equally.

Some founders sell too early and miss enormous upside potential. Others hold too long and watch valuations collapse. Some lose substantial wealth through poor tax planning. Others become trapped by lock-up agreements, poor legal structuring, or unfavorable deal terms. Some founders achieve large exits but fail to preserve wealth afterward because they never developed long-term financial management strategies.

This book will help explain how founders can approach

liquidity strategically rather than emotionally.

It will also examine how wealth is often built in stages rather than through a single massive exit. Many successful entrepreneurs create partial liquidity over time. They may sell small ownership percentages during private rounds, secondary transactions, recapitalizations, or public market offerings while continuing to retain substantial upside ownership. This allows founders to reduce personal financial pressure while still participating in future company growth.

One of the most important psychological transformations for entrepreneurs occurs when they stop thinking purely like operators and begin thinking like capital allocators.

At the beginning of a startup journey, founders are often focused entirely on survival. They focus on customers, revenue generation, payroll, product development, and operational growth. But as companies scale, founders must also learn how capital markets work. They must understand investor psychology, valuation mechanics, institutional capital behavior, public market expectations, and wealth preservation strategies.

Founders who fail to make this transition often struggle during major growth stages.

Building a successful company requires one set of skills. Managing equity wealth requires another.

Throughout this book, you will learn how founders create wealth through multiple types of equity events. You will explore IPOs, acquisitions, mergers, venture capital exits, secondary transactions, stock compensation structures, strategic buyouts, and public market liquidity opportunities. You will also examine how company valuation affects founder wealth and how market timing can dramatically impact outcomes.

Another major theme of this book is the relationship between control and wealth.

Some founders prioritize maintaining total control over their companies. Others prioritize rapid scaling through external capital. Neither approach is universally correct. Every founder must determine the balance between ownership, control, growth speed, dilution, and long-term financial goals.

In some cases, maintaining majority ownership may preserve independence and decision-making power. In other cases, partnering with institutional investors may accelerate growth so dramatically that overall wealth creation becomes exponentially larger despite lower ownership percentages. The most successful founders understand that ownership strategy is not emotional. It is mathematical, strategic, and deeply connected to long-term vision.

This book will also explore founder stock structures, voting rights, dual-class shares, preferred equity, common stock, employee stock options, vesting schedules, and anti-dilution protections. These structures may seem technical at first, but they play a major role in determining how wealth is ultimately distributed within a company.

A founder who understands equity structure gains leverage.

A founder who ignores it risks losing leverage.

One of the reasons founder wealth creation is so fascinating is because capital markets reward scalability at extraordinary levels. Public markets often value companies not only based on current profits but also based on future growth potential, recurring revenue predictability, market dominance, technological advantage, network effects, and investor confidence.

This creates enormous opportunities for founders who build scalable systems.

A founder who creates a software company with recurring subscription revenue may achieve dramatically higher valuations than a traditional local business with similar annual profits. A media company with scalable digital distribution may command higher valuation multiples than a labor-intensive service business. A platform company with strong network effects may experience exponential valuation growth as adoption increases.

Understanding these dynamics helps founders position companies strategically for future wealth creation opportunities.

This book is not only about billion-dollar technology startups. The principles of equity wealth creation apply across many industries. Real estate businesses, education companies, SaaS platforms, financial firms, healthcare companies, manufacturing operations, media brands, AI companies, franchise systems, and digital businesses can all create meaningful founder wealth when structured correctly.

What matters most is understanding how enterprise value is built and how ownership participates in that value creation.

The entrepreneurs who build lasting wealth are often those who think beyond immediate income and begin focusing on long-term enterprise appreciation. They understand that equity can become one of the greatest wealth-building tools ever created when combined with vision, patience, execution, and intelligent capital strategy. As you move through this book, you will begin seeing business ownership differently. You will start recognizing how founders structure companies for future exits, how investors evaluate ownership opportunities, how liquidity events are engineered, and how sophisticated entrepreneurs convert company growth into long-term personal financial freedom.

You will also learn that founder wealth creation is not solely about money. Ownership creates leverage, freedom, opportunity, influence, and long-term flexibility. It allows founders to reinvest into new ventures, support future generations, fund philanthropy, acquire additional businesses, diversify assets, and create entirely new ecosystems of opportunity.

Many of the world's most influential entrepreneurs achieved freedom not because they worked harder than everyone else, but because they understood ownership better than everyone else.

That is the purpose of this book.

This book is designed to help you understand how founder wealth is truly created, protected, scaled, and transformed through equity events and capital market opportunities. Whether your goal is to eventually take a company public, attract institutional investment, engineer a strategic acquisition, build long-term recurring wealth, or simply understand how ownership creates financial leverage, the principles inside these chapters can help reshape how you think about business and wealth creation itself.

The future belongs to founders who understand not only how to build companies, but how to build ownership structures that create lasting value long after the original business is launched.

Welcome to Founder Wealth Creation Through Equity Events.

Chapter 1

Understanding Founder Equity and the Psychology of Ownership

The foundation of nearly every major entrepreneurial fortune in modern history begins with a single concept: ownership. While most people spend their lives exchanging time for money through salaries, wages, commissions, or service-based income, founders who understand equity operate within a completely different financial framework. Instead of focusing only on what they earn today, they focus on what they own tomorrow. This distinction changes how businesses are built, how decisions are made, and how wealth is ultimately created over the long term.

Founder equity represents ownership in a company. It is the financial and strategic interest a founder holds in the business they create. This ownership may begin at one hundred percent when a company is first formed, but over time it often evolves through investment rounds, partnerships, employee stock grants, mergers, acquisitions, and public offerings. The key principle is that ownership gives founders participation in the growth and value creation of the business itself. As the company becomes more valuable, the founder's ownership stake may become significantly more valuable as well. Many entrepreneurs initially focus heavily on revenue and income because those metrics feel immediate and measurable. Revenue pays bills. Income supports lifestyles. Cash flow keeps businesses alive. Yet the entrepreneurs who ultimately create extraordinary wealth often understand that enterprise value and ownership appreciation can dramatically exceed traditional income over time. A founder who earns a modest salary while building a rapidly appreciating company may eventually create far greater wealth than someone earning a large salary with no ownership in scalable assets.

This shift in thinking is one of the most important psychological transitions in entrepreneurship. Employees are often conditioned to think in terms of compensation. Founders must learn to think in terms of valuation, ownership leverage, scalability, and equity appreciation. This mindset change requires patience because equity wealth is usually not immediate. It compounds over years of execution, growth, strategic positioning, and market expansion.

The psychology of ownership changes behavior. When founders truly understand that every improvement in the company increases the value of their ownership stake, their perspective evolves dramatically. Decisions become more strategic. Long-term planning becomes more important. Brand reputation, operational systems, recurring revenue, customer retention, intellectual property, and scalability all begin to matter more because they influence future valuation potential.

This is one reason many successful founders willingly reinvest profits back into growth rather than extracting all available cash from the business. They recognize that increasing enterprise value can generate exponentially larger long-term wealth opportunities. While short-term income may temporarily decrease due to reinvestment, the long-term value of ownership may increase dramatically.

For example, a founder who owns a software company generating recurring subscription revenue may choose to aggressively expand marketing, improve technology, hire talent, and scale operations even if short-term profits decline. Why? Because the founder understands that recurring revenue businesses often receive higher valuation multiples in private and public markets. Increasing growth velocity, customer retention, and market dominance may increase the eventual enterprise value far beyond the temporary reduction in short-term profits.

This type of thinking separates operators from wealth builders.

Many small business owners unknowingly trap themselves because they structure companies entirely around personal income extraction rather than enterprise value creation. They prioritize immediate cash flow at the expense of scalability. They avoid delegation, underinvest in systems, refuse to build management teams, and fail to create repeatable operational structures. As a result, the business becomes heavily dependent on the owner personally. This limits valuation because buyers and investors prefer businesses that can operate independently of a single individual.

Founder wealth creation requires building assets that have transferable value.

This means creating businesses that can scale beyond the founder's direct labor. It means developing systems, processes, intellectual property, brands, customer bases, recurring revenue streams, and operational infrastructure that investors or buyers view as durable and valuable. Equity becomes more valuable when the business itself becomes more scalable, stable, and attractive to future capital providers.

Another important aspect of founder psychology involves risk tolerance. Traditional employment generally provides predictable income and lower financial uncertainty. Entrepreneurship often involves volatility, delayed rewards, uncertainty, and emotional stress. Founders may work for years without significant personal financial rewards while reinvesting capital back into growth. This requires emotional resilience and belief in long-term ownership value. Some of the world's largest founder fortunes were built because entrepreneurs tolerated short-term uncertainty in exchange for long-term equity appreciation. They delayed gratification. They focused on building value rather than maximizing immediate compensation. They accepted temporary sacrifices because they believed in the future potential of their ownership stake.

However, this approach also requires balance. Founders who neglect personal financial stability entirely may experience excessive pressure that eventually affects decision-making quality. Financial stress can create desperation, emotional decisions, or premature exits. This is why many sophisticated founders eventually seek partial liquidity opportunities during growth stages. By selling a small percentage of shares through secondary transactions or recapitalizations, founders can reduce personal financial pressure while still maintaining substantial ownership upside.

Understanding this balance between long-term equity growth and personal financial stability is extremely important.

One of the greatest emotional challenges founders face is dilution anxiety. When investors enter a company, founders typically exchange ownership percentages for capital. Many entrepreneurs instinctively resist dilution because they fear losing control or reducing future wealth potential. While protecting ownership is important, dilution itself is not automatically negative.

What matters most is whether the overall value of ownership increases.

A founder who owns one hundred percent of a company valued at one million dollars technically controls one million dollars in equity value. But a founder who owns fifteen percent of a company valued at two billion dollars controls vastly greater wealth despite owning a smaller percentage. Sophisticated founders understand that strategic dilution can become a wealth multiplication tool when external capital accelerates growth dramatically.

This concept is one of the most misunderstood areas of entrepreneurship.

Many inexperienced founders focus too heavily on percentage ownership while ignoring enterprise value growth. Institutional investors, venture capital firms, and private equity groups often provide far more than money alone. They may provide networks, strategic guidance, talent recruitment assistance, credibility, partnerships, operational expertise, acquisition opportunities, and access to future capital markets. When these resources accelerate growth significantly, founder wealth can increase dramatically even after dilution. At the same time, founders must also protect themselves from unnecessary or excessive dilution. Poorly negotiated fundraising rounds, weak legal structures, poorly designed stock option pools, and unfavorable liquidation preferences can severely reduce founder wealth over time. This is why understanding cap tables, shareholder agreements, voting rights, anti-dilution clauses, and financing structures becomes critical.

Founder equity is not only about ownership quantity. It is also about ownership quality.

Sophisticated founders think strategically about how ownership rights are structured. Some founders create dual-class share structures that allow them to retain voting control even after selling large ownership percentages. Others negotiate protective provisions that preserve decision-making authority during fundraising rounds. Some founders intentionally structure vesting schedules and stock option plans to attract top talent while minimizing unnecessary dilution.

Ownership structure affects power.

Power affects decision-making.

Decision-making affects long-term value creation.

Another major psychological shift occurs when founders begin understanding that valuation is often driven by perception as much as performance. Investors do not simply analyze current financial results. They evaluate future growth potential, scalability, market size, leadership quality, competitive positioning, recurring revenue predictability, margins, technology advantages, and strategic opportunity.

This means founders must learn how markets think.

Building a valuable company is partly operational and partly psychological. Public markets and institutional investors reward confidence, vision, growth narratives, scalability, and long-term opportunity. Founders who understand this begin focusing heavily on positioning, investor communication, storytelling, and strategic branding in addition to operational execution.

This does not mean exaggerating or misleading investors. It means understanding how sophisticated capital evaluates future potential.

For example, two businesses generating similar profits may receive dramatically different valuations depending on industry, scalability, growth trajectory, recurring revenue, margins, and future expansion opportunities. A software company with recurring subscriptions may receive far higher valuation multiples than a local service business because investors believe future growth potential is greater.

This understanding changes founder behavior.

Instead of focusing solely on present income, founders begin building companies that markets perceive as scalable assets. They optimize for long-term enterprise value creation rather than short-term extraction.

Another important element of founder psychology is identity attachment. Many entrepreneurs become emotionally attached to their companies because the business represents years of sacrifice, creativity, ambition, and personal struggle. While passion can drive exceptional execution, excessive emotional attachment can also create problems.

Some founders refuse acquisitions because they emotionally identify too strongly with ownership. Others reject strategic partnerships that could accelerate growth. Some fail to replace themselves operationally because they believe the business cannot function without them. These behaviors can limit scalability and reduce future valuation.

Sophisticated founders learn how to separate ego from strategy.

They understand that wealth creation often requires adaptability, delegation, partnership, and long-term planning. They recognize that building enterprise value may require organizational evolution beyond the founder's direct involvement.

This becomes especially important during major liquidity events.

Acquisitions, IPOs, mergers, and recapitalizations can create enormous founder wealth, but they also involve emotional complexity. Founders may suddenly transition from operators to shareholders. They may experience public scrutiny, investor pressure, regulatory obligations, or changing leadership dynamics. Understanding the emotional side of ownership helps founders navigate these transitions more effectively.

Another major concept in founder wealth creation is time horizon expansion.

Most people think in short financial cycles. They focus on weekly income, monthly bills, yearly salaries, or quarterly results. Wealthy founders often think in decades. They understand that enterprise value compounds over time. Brand equity compounds. Customer relationships compound. Technology infrastructure compounds. Intellectual property compounds. Market dominance compounds.

Patience becomes a strategic advantage.

Many founders who achieve major exits spent years building systems before receiving significant liquidity. Their wealth was not created overnight even if the public perceives it that way. In reality, large equity outcomes are often the result of long-term compounding combined with strategic execution and market timing.

This long-term perspective also changes how founders evaluate setbacks.

Temporary losses, operational challenges, market volatility, failed product launches, and economic downturns become part of a larger journey rather than catastrophic endpoints. Founders who understand ownership psychology often maintain stronger resilience because they focus on long-term enterprise value rather than short-term fluctuations.

The most successful founders eventually realize that equity ownership is one of the most powerful wealth-building tools in existence because it allows them to participate in scalable growth far beyond personal labor limitations. Ownership creates leverage. A founder can sleep while the company continues generating revenue, expanding customers, building technology, and increasing value.

This is fundamentally different from linear income.

Linear income requires continuous labor input. Equity ownership allows wealth to grow through enterprise appreciation. This distinction is at the center of modern founder wealth creation.

As companies scale, founders also begin understanding the importance of liquidity planning. Equity may appear valuable on paper, but paper wealth and realized wealth are not the same thing. Sophisticated founders eventually learn how to strategically convert portions of equity into diversified assets, investments, cash reserves, and long-term wealth preservation structures without destroying future upside potential.

This is where entrepreneurship intersects with capital markets.

Founders who master both business building and ownership strategy place themselves in a position to create extraordinary long-term wealth. They learn how to think like operators during growth phases and like investors during liquidity phases. They understand that wealth creation is not accidental.

It is engineered through intentional ownership strategy, disciplined execution, strategic capital allocation, and long-term vision.

Ultimately, founder equity is about far more than shares in a company. It represents participation in value creation itself. It rewards innovation, scalability, leadership, vision, and persistence. It transforms businesses into financial assets capable of generating generational wealth. The entrepreneurs who understand ownership psychology gain a massive advantage because they stop viewing businesses only as jobs and start viewing them as wealth-building ecosystems. They begin building not just for income, but for enterprise value, scalability, leverage, and long-term financial freedom.

That transformation changes everything.

The Founder Who Stopped Chasing Income

Daniel Ruiz spent most of his early adult life believing success meant earning more money every year. Like many ambitious professionals, he measured progress through salary increases, bonuses, commissions, and visible lifestyle improvements. He graduated from college with average grades but extraordinary determination, and by the age of twenty-eight he had already built a respectable career in software sales. His income had climbed steadily, and on the surface his life looked impressive.

He leased a luxury car, rented a high-rise apartment, traveled frequently, and wore expensive watches that symbolized what he believed success should look like.

Yet despite earning more money than most of his friends, Daniel constantly felt trapped.

Every month required more income to maintain the life he had built. Every promotion increased expectations. Every raise disappeared into new expenses. He worked longer hours each year, but true financial freedom always seemed distant. Deep down, he knew he was building income but not wealth.

Everything began changing after an unexpected conversation with one of his clients.

The client was a quiet founder named Rebecca Hall, who operated a small but rapidly growing SaaS company specializing in logistics automation. Daniel initially assumed Rebecca was under financial pressure because her salary appeared surprisingly low compared to the scale of her business operations. During one meeting, Daniel casually asked why she paid herself less than many mid-level corporate employees despite running a growing company.

Rebecca smiled and asked a question Daniel never forgot.

"Do you want income, or do you want ownership?"

At first, Daniel did not fully understand what she meant. Rebecca explained that while she intentionally kept her salary modest, she owned a large percentage of a company that had doubled in value nearly every year for the past four years. Investors had recently valued her company at over sixty million dollars. Although her yearly salary was less than Daniel's commissions, her ownership stake represented life-changing wealth potential. That conversation disrupted Daniel's entire financial philosophy.

For weeks afterward, he could not stop thinking about the difference between earning money and owning assets. He began studying founders, IPOs, acquisitions, and startup equity structures late at night after work. He realized that many of the wealthiest entrepreneurs in the world were not necessarily the highest-paid employees. They were owners of scalable assets.

The realization both inspired and terrified him.

Daniel had spent years optimizing for short-term income. Ownership felt uncertain, risky, and uncomfortable. Building a company required sacrifice, delayed gratification, and emotional resilience. Yet he also understood something important for the first time: his current path had limitations.

No matter how high his salary climbed, he was still trading time for money.

Six months later, Daniel made one of the most difficult decisions of his life. He left his stable sales career and partnered with a software engineer named Marcus to launch a business analytics platform for small logistics companies. The early months were brutal. Revenue was inconsistent. Cash reserves disappeared quickly. Daniel sold his luxury car, moved into a smaller apartment, and drastically reduced his lifestyle expenses.

Friends questioned his decision constantly.

Some thought he was having a crisis. Others believed he was throwing away a successful career for a fantasy. Daniel himself questioned the decision many nights when payroll deadlines approached and customer growth slowed.

But something inside him had changed.

For the first time in his life, he felt connected to ownership instead of temporary income. Every new customer increased enterprise value. Every product improvement strengthened the company. Every recurring subscription contract expanded long-term scalability. Even though his personal income had decreased dramatically, he felt more optimistic about the future than ever before.

Years passed.

The company slowly gained traction. Then growth accelerated.

A major transportation firm signed a national licensing agreement that transformed the business overnight. Investors began reaching out. Venture capital firms requested meetings. Industry publications featured the company as an emerging logistics technology leader. Suddenly, Daniel found himself sitting in rooms with institutional investors discussing valuations that once seemed impossible.

The first investment offer shocked him emotionally.

One venture capital firm offered twenty million dollars in funding in exchange for twenty-five percent ownership. Younger Daniel would have panicked at the idea of giving away part of the company. But by now Daniel understood enterprise value. He realized that owning a smaller percentage of a rapidly scaling company could create far greater wealth than maintaining total ownership of a smaller operation.

After months of negotiation, the deal closed.

The capital transformed the business. The company hired engineers, expanded internationally, improved infrastructure, and accelerated product development. Revenue exploded over the next three years.

Daniel's paper wealth climbed dramatically.

But despite the rising valuation, he still faced personal financial pressure because most of his wealth remained illiquid. His ownership stake looked impressive on spreadsheets, yet much of his lifestyle remained conservative because the equity could not easily be converted into usable cash. This created a new psychological challenge.

Outsiders assumed Daniel was wealthy because industry articles discussed the company's valuation publicly. Yet his actual liquid financial resources were still relatively modest compared to the paper value of his ownership. He finally understood why so many founders feel emotionally conflicted during growth stages.

Then came the acquisition offer.

One of the world's largest enterprise software companies approached them privately with a multi-billion-dollar acquisition proposal. The numbers felt surreal. Daniel barely slept during the negotiation process. Accepting the deal would create generational wealth. Rejecting it could potentially lead to even larger future growth through an IPO.

The decision consumed him emotionally.

For weeks he struggled with identity attachment. The company represented nearly a decade of sacrifice, struggle, vision, and personal transformation. Selling felt strangely emotional, almost like giving away part of himself.

Marcus eventually said something that changed Daniel's perspective.

"We didn't build this company to own it forever. We built it to create value." That sentence clarified everything.

Daniel realized he had unconsciously attached his identity too tightly to ownership itself instead of the purpose behind ownership. Wealth creation was not about clinging emotionally to shares forever. It was about creating value strategically and then using that value to create freedom, opportunity, and future impact.

The acquisition closed eight months later.

For the first time in his life, Daniel experienced true financial freedom. Yet the most surprising part was not the money itself. It was the realization that wealth had been built gradually through ownership psychology long before the acquisition occurred.

The real transformation happened years earlier when he stopped thinking like an employee and started thinking like an owner.

After the acquisition, Daniel diversified his wealth carefully. He invested in startups, real estate, private equity opportunities, and long-term market investments. He funded educational initiatives for young entrepreneurs and began mentoring founders navigating early growth stages.

During mentorship sessions, he noticed many new entrepreneurs repeating the same mistake he once made. They obsessed over short-term income while ignoring long-term ownership value.

Daniel often asked them the same question Rebecca once asked him.

"Do you want income, or do you want ownership?"

Most people answered too quickly.

The founders who paused before responding were usually the ones most likely to understand the deeper meaning behind the question.

Because true founder wealth is rarely built through immediate rewards.

It is built through patience, scalability, ownership, leverage, and the willingness to think beyond today's paycheck toward tomorrow's enterprise value.

And once a founder truly understands that difference, their entire relationship with business, money, and opportunity changes forever.

Chapter 2

Stock Dilution, Ownership Structures, and Long-Term Wealth Preservation

One of the most important—and most misunderstood—concepts in founder wealth creation is dilution. Many entrepreneurs enter the business world with a simple assumption: owning a larger percentage of a company automatically means greater wealth. While ownership percentage certainly matters, sophisticated founders eventually learn that the true objective is not merely preserving percentage ownership. The real objective is maximizing the long-term value of ownership over time.

This distinction changes everything.

A founder who owns one hundred percent of a small company worth one million dollars controls one million dollars in equity value. However, a founder who owns ten percent of a company worth five billion dollars controls dramatically more wealth despite holding a much smaller ownership percentage. This simple mathematical reality explains why dilution, when managed strategically, can become one of the most powerful wealth-creation tools available to entrepreneurs.

Understanding dilution begins with understanding

capitalization structures.

Every company has a cap table, or capitalization table, that outlines ownership distribution among founders, investors, employees, advisors, and other shareholders. In the earliest stages of a business, founders often own nearly all outstanding shares. Over time, however, additional shares may be issued to investors, employees, strategic partners, or institutions. As new shares are created, the ownership percentages of existing shareholders may decline. This process is known as dilution.

For inexperienced founders, dilution often feels emotionally threatening. Entrepreneurs may fear losing control, reducing future wealth, or weakening decision-making authority. These fears are understandable because ownership represents not only financial value but also emotional investment, identity, sacrifice, and years of hard work. However, sophisticated founders learn to evaluate dilution strategically rather than emotionally.

The critical question is not simply whether dilution occurs.

The critical question is whether the value created through dilution exceeds the ownership percentage surrendered.

For example, imagine a founder owns one hundred percent of a startup valued at two million dollars. The founder then accepts venture capital funding that reduces ownership to seventy percent but increases company valuation to twenty million dollars through accelerated growth, hiring, technology expansion, and market penetration. Despite dilution, the founder's actual equity value increases substantially because the overall enterprise becomes far more valuable.

This principle sits at the center of modern startup financing.

External capital can dramatically accelerate company growth. Venture capital firms, private equity groups, institutional investors, strategic corporate investors, and public markets often provide resources that founders cannot access independently. These resources may include growth capital, strategic guidance, hiring support, industry relationships, operational expertise, acquisition opportunities, international expansion pathways, and credibility within capital markets.

When used intelligently, these advantages can increase enterprise value exponentially.

However, dilution can also become dangerous when founders fail to understand financing structures properly. Poorly negotiated investment terms, unnecessary fundraising rounds, excessive option pools, unfavorable liquidation preferences, or poorly timed capital raises can severely reduce long-term founder wealth. This is why understanding ownership structure is essential for long-term wealth preservation.

One of the first major financing decisions many founders face involves seed-stage fundraising. In early startup environments, entrepreneurs often exchange equity for capital because traditional bank financing is unavailable or impractical. Early-stage investors take substantial risks because most startups fail. As compensation for that risk, investors typically receive ownership stakes at relatively low valuations.

At this stage, valuation becomes extremely important.

A founder who raises one million dollars at a five million dollar valuation gives away significantly more ownership than a founder who raises one million dollars at a twenty million dollar valuation. This means founders must balance capital needs carefully. Raising too little money may limit growth. Raising too much too early may create unnecessary dilution.

Sophisticated founders learn that capital efficiency matters.

Investors evaluate not only growth potential but also how effectively founders deploy resources. Companies that demonstrate strong operational efficiency often gain negotiating leverage during future fundraising rounds because investors perceive lower risk and higher execution quality.

Another important concept is pre-money and post-money valuation.

Pre-money valuation refers to the company's estimated value before investment capital enters the business. Post-money valuation includes the new investment capital. Understanding this distinction is critical because ownership percentages are calculated based on post-money valuation structures.

For example, if a company has a pre-money valuation of ten million dollars and raises two million dollars from investors, the post-money valuation becomes twelve million dollars. The investors would own approximately sixteen point seven percent of the company after the investment closes.

These calculations directly affect founder ownership.

As companies grow through multiple fundraising rounds, dilution compounds. Seed rounds may be followed by Series A, Series B, Series C, growth equity rounds, secondary transactions, convertible debt conversions, strategic investments, and eventually public offerings. Each stage potentially reduces founder ownership percentages further.

Yet many of the world's wealthiest founders still retained extraordinary wealth despite significant dilution because enterprise value increased dramatically throughout the process.

This reveals another critical principle: valuation growth can outweigh dilution.

The most successful founders focus not only on ownership percentage but also on valuation trajectory. They understand that smaller percentages of massive enterprises often create far greater wealth than majority ownership in limited-growth businesses.

However, maintaining thoughtful ownership structure still matters tremendously.

One major concern founders face is control dilution. Ownership percentages do not simply affect financial outcomes. They also affect governance, voting rights, strategic authority, board influence, and operational control. A founder who becomes excessively diluted may lose the ability to direct the company's future.

This is why governance structures become critically important.

Some founders implement dual-class share structures that preserve voting control even after ownership percentages decline. Under these systems, founders may hold shares with enhanced voting rights while public investors or institutions hold standard voting shares. Several major technology companies used this structure to allow founders to maintain long-term strategic influence while accessing public market capital.

These structures remain controversial in some financial circles because they concentrate power among founders. However, supporters argue that they protect long-term innovation by insulating visionary leaders from short-term market pressure.

Regardless of structure, founders must understand the relationship between ownership and control.

Another essential area of ownership structure involves employee stock options.

Many high-growth companies use equity compensation to attract talented employees when cash resources are limited. Engineers, executives, designers, sales leaders, and operational managers may receive stock options or restricted stock units as part of compensation packages. This aligns employee incentives with company growth because team members participate financially in future success.

While option pools dilute founder ownership, they can also significantly increase enterprise value by attracting world-class talent.

Again, the goal is intelligent dilution rather than emotional resistance to all dilution. Sophisticated founders carefully evaluate how much equity to allocate toward employee incentive programs. Strong talent can dramatically increase company valuation, accelerate growth, improve innovation, and strengthen operational scalability. In many cases, strategic employee equity distribution becomes one of the best long-term investments a founder can make.

Another major concept founders must understand is liquidation preference.

Liquidation preferences determine how proceeds are distributed during acquisitions, mergers, or company sales. Some investors negotiate terms guaranteeing they recover their investment capital before founders receive proceeds. More aggressive terms may include multiple liquidation preferences or participating preferred structures, which can dramatically reduce founder payouts during exits.

Many inexperienced founders focus heavily on headline valuation numbers while ignoring liquidation structures hidden within financing agreements.

This can become catastrophic.

A company may appear highly valuable publicly, but founders may discover during an acquisition that investor preferences absorb much of the proceeds before common shareholders participate meaningfully. This is why founders must understand legal agreements thoroughly and work with experienced advisors during fundraising negotiations.

Ownership preservation also involves avoiding unnecessary dilution through operational discipline.

Some companies raise excessive capital prematurely because founders pursue vanity valuations, media attention, or unsustainable growth expectations. Large fundraising rounds may temporarily increase company valuation but also create pressure for unrealistic expansion and future financing dependency.

Founders who maintain strong financial discipline often preserve greater ownership over time.

Companies with healthy margins, efficient operations, recurring revenue, and predictable cash flow frequently gain flexibility. They may choose when to raise capital rather than being forced into financing due to cash shortages. This negotiating leverage can significantly improve long-term ownership outcomes.

Timing also plays a critical role in dilution management.

Raising capital during periods of strong growth, favorable market conditions, and positive investor sentiment often leads to higher valuations and lower dilution. Conversely, companies raising money during financial distress, economic downturns, or operational instability may face severe dilution because investors perceive elevated risk.

Sophisticated founders therefore think strategically about timing fundraising events.

They build relationships with investors before capital becomes urgently necessary. They monitor market conditions carefully. They position the company attractively through operational milestones, customer growth, profitability improvements, and strategic momentum before entering financing discussions.

Another important area of wealth preservation involves secondary transactions.

As companies scale, founders sometimes sell small portions of their ownership privately before major liquidity events like IPOs or acquisitions. This allows founders to reduce personal financial pressure while maintaining substantial upside participation.

Secondary liquidity can improve founder psychology significantly.

Entrepreneurs who remain entirely illiquid for many years may experience extreme emotional stress because personal finances become heavily dependent on uncertain future outcomes. Partial liquidity allows founders to diversify assets, reduce financial anxiety, support families, and make long-term decisions more rationally.

However, founders must approach secondary transactions carefully because excessive early selling may signal weak confidence to investors or reduce future upside participation.

Balance is essential.

Wealth preservation also requires understanding taxes.

Many founders focus intensely on valuation growth while ignoring future tax implications. Capital gains taxes, stock option taxation, QSBS rules, estate planning structures, charitable trusts, and geographic tax considerations can dramatically affect final wealth outcomes.

Sophisticated founders begin planning tax strategy long before liquidity events occur.

They work with legal advisors, accountants, estate planners, and wealth managers to structure ownership intelligently. Proper planning can preserve enormous amounts of wealth over time.

Another critical area of long-term wealth preservation is diversification. Many founders become excessively concentrated in a single asset: their company stock. While concentration may create wealth initially, long-term preservation often requires diversification after liquidity events. Public market volatility, industry disruption, technological change, regulatory shifts, or competitive pressure can reduce company value dramatically.

Founders who gradually diversify after major liquidity events often preserve wealth more effectively across generations.

This transition from wealth creation to wealth preservation represents another major psychological shift.

Entrepreneurs are often trained to take risks aggressively during growth stages. However, preserving large-scale wealth frequently requires different behaviors including risk management, asset allocation, tax efficiency, estate planning, and long-term capital preservation.

The most successful founders understand both sides of this equation.

They know when to take concentrated risks during company-building phases and when to diversify strategically after liquidity events occur.

Ultimately, dilution itself is neither inherently good nor inherently bad. Dilution is a tool.

When used intelligently, it can accelerate growth, increase enterprise value, attract elite talent, strengthen market positioning, and create extraordinary founder wealth. When handled poorly, it can destroy control, reduce long-term ownership value, weaken incentives, and undermine future financial outcomes.

The key is intentionality.

Sophisticated founders approach ownership structures strategically. They understand valuation mathematics, governance dynamics, financing structures, investor incentives, and long-term wealth planning. They recognize that ownership is not merely emotional. It is structural, financial, legal, psychological, and deeply connected to future freedom.

Founders who master these concepts gain one of the greatest advantages in entrepreneurship: the ability to grow aggressively while preserving long-term wealth intelligently.

That balance often determines whether a founder simply builds a successful company—or creates lasting generational wealth.

The Founder Who Almost Lost Everything

Sophia Martinez stared silently at the ownership spreadsheet glowing on her laptop screen late one Friday night. The office was empty except for the quiet hum of servers and the distant sound of traffic outside the downtown windows. Three years earlier, she had launched her cybersecurity startup from a small apartment with little more than determination, technical expertise, and relentless ambition. Now the company was valued at nearly one hundred million dollars.

Yet as she examined the cap table carefully, a terrifying realization began sinking in.

Despite building the company from scratch, her ownership percentage had fallen dramatically through multiple fundraising rounds. What once started as nearly full ownership had slowly shrunk through seed financing, employee option pools, strategic partnerships, and institutional investment deals.

Sophia suddenly understood something that no one had fully explained during the excitement of growth.

Valuation alone did not guarantee founder wealth.

The realization shook her emotionally because from the outside, her life appeared wildly successful. Financial media outlets praised her as a rising technology founder. Venture capital firms competed for meetings. Industry conferences invited her to speak about scaling cybersecurity infrastructure. Employees viewed her as visionary leadership. But privately, Sophia felt increasingly anxious.

Every funding round had seemed logical at the time. Investors promised accelerated growth. Advisors emphasized market expansion opportunities. Recruiters insisted elite talent required larger option pools. Board members pushed aggressive scaling strategies to dominate competitors quickly.

And to be fair, much of it had worked.

Revenue exploded. Customer acquisition accelerated. Enterprise clients signed massive contracts. The company expanded internationally faster than anyone expected. Yet hidden beneath the momentum was a growing complexity surrounding ownership and control.

Sophia remembered the early days vividly.

At twenty-nine years old, she had left a stable corporate cybersecurity position because she believed companies desperately needed simpler AI-driven threat detection systems. She spent nights coding prototypes and days pitching potential clients. During those first months, survival mattered more than ownership structure.

When the first investor offered one million dollars in seed capital, Sophia barely negotiated. She felt grateful anyone believed in her vision. At the time, surrendering twenty percent ownership seemed insignificant compared to gaining resources to survive.

Then came the Series A round.

The company needed engineers, marketing infrastructure, compliance systems, and enterprise-level servers. Investors pushed for aggressive expansion. Another large ownership percentage disappeared during negotiations.

Then came the Series B.

By then the startup ecosystem treated Sophia like a rising star. Growth expectations intensified. Investors demanded faster hiring, larger marketing budgets, international offices, and acquisition discussions.

The company kept growing.

So did the dilution.

At first Sophia ignored the numbers because the valuation increases felt exciting. Headlines celebrated the company's rising worth. But eventually she began understanding the difference between enterprise valuation and personal ownership value.

The moment of clarity came during a private board meeting. One institutional investor casually mentioned that future financing rounds could potentially reduce founder ownership below ten percent before a public offering. The comment hit Sophia like a punch to the chest.

Below ten percent.

That night she stayed alone in the office reviewing every financing agreement she had signed over the years. For the first time, she studied liquidation preferences carefully. She analyzed voting structures. She reviewed employee option expansion terms. She calculated how future rounds might affect her ownership if growth targets were missed.

The numbers frightened her.

Although her remaining ownership was still valuable, she realized how easily founders could lose leverage if they failed to understand financing structures deeply.

Sophia barely slept that weekend.

Monday morning, she contacted an experienced attorney specializing in founder equity strategy. Over several intense meetings, the attorney explained concepts Sophia wished she had fully understood years earlier: protective provisions, anti-dilution mechanics, governance structures, secondary liquidity planning, and voting control systems. The conversations transformed her perspective completely.

For the first time, Sophia stopped viewing ownership emotionally and started viewing it strategically.

She realized dilution itself was not automatically the enemy. The company truly had become far more valuable because of external capital and accelerated growth. Without investors, the business likely would never have scaled globally. But she also realized that intelligent founders actively manage ownership structure throughout the company lifecycle rather than reacting passively during financing rounds.

That realization marked a turning point.

During the next fundraising process, Sophia approached negotiations differently. Instead of focusing only on valuation, she prioritized governance structure, voting protections, and long-term ownership planning. She negotiated more carefully around liquidation preferences and employee equity expansion. She built stronger relationships with legal and financial advisors who understood founder wealth preservation.

Most importantly, she began thinking long term.

Rather than endlessly chasing higher valuations, Sophia started evaluating whether each financing decision genuinely strengthened enterprise value or merely created temporary momentum. Around that same time, another opportunity emerged.

A private secondary market firm approached Sophia with an offer to purchase a small percentage of her personal shares. Initially, she resisted emotionally because selling shares felt like weakening her belief in the company.

But her advisors challenged her thinking.

They explained that partial liquidity could reduce financial stress without meaningfully reducing long-term upside. After years of living modestly while building a rapidly growing company, Sophia's entire personal financial future remained tied almost entirely to one illiquid asset.

Eventually, she agreed to sell a very small portion of her ownership.

The transaction changed her psychology immediately.

For the first time in years, Sophia felt emotionally stable. She paid off family debts, purchased a home for her parents, diversified investments modestly, and created personal financial security independent of future company uncertainty.

Ironically, the reduced pressure made her a better CEO.

Because she no longer felt financially desperate, her decision-making became calmer, more strategic, and less emotional. She focused more clearly on long-term enterprise building instead of short-term valuation obsession.

Years later, the company successfully completed a public offering.

The IPO generated extraordinary wealth for employees, investors, and early stakeholders. Financial media celebrated

Sophia as one of the most successful cybersecurity founders of her generation.

But privately, Sophia understood something deeper than most observers realized.

The real victory was not simply the IPO itself.

The real victory was learning how to balance growth with ownership preservation before it was too late.

Many founders build valuable companies.

Far fewer understand how to preserve meaningful long-term wealth while scaling aggressively.

Sophia eventually became known among younger entrepreneurs not only for building a successful company, but for openly teaching founders about ownership structure, dilution psychology, and wealth preservation strategy. During mentorship sessions, founders often asked her whether dilution was dangerous.

Sophia always gave the same answer.

“Bad dilution destroys founders. Smart dilution creates empires.”

Then she would pause before adding the lesson that changed her own life forever.

"But only if you understand the difference before the paperwork is signed."

Chapter 3

Liquidity Events and How Founders Convert Equity Into Real Wealth

One of the greatest misconceptions in entrepreneurship is the belief that valuation automatically equals wealth. In reality, there is a massive difference between paper wealth and realized wealth. A founder may own shares in a company valued at hundreds of millions or even billions of dollars, yet still have limited access to actual usable capital if those shares remain illiquid. This distinction is one of the most important concepts in founder wealth creation.

Liquidity is the process through which ownership becomes convertible into cash or marketable financial assets.

A liquidity event occurs when founders, investors, employees, or shareholders gain the ability to sell or monetize their equity holdings. These events often represent the financial culmination of years of sacrifice, execution, risk-taking, and long-term company building. While the public often focuses on valuations and headlines, sophisticated founders understand that liquidity strategy is where theoretical wealth becomes practical wealth. This transition changes lives. For many entrepreneurs, the early stages of company building involve uncertainty, personal financial sacrifices, delayed gratification, and immense pressure. Founders may spend years reinvesting profits into growth while paying themselves modest salaries. Their wealth may exist largely on spreadsheets rather than in accessible bank accounts. Liquidity events can transform this dynamic by allowing founders to finally access the value they helped create.

However, liquidity events are far more complex than simply "selling a company."

Different liquidity structures create different financial outcomes, tax consequences, control dynamics, emotional pressures, and long-term wealth opportunities. Understanding these structures is critical because the way founders approach liquidity can significantly affect the amount of wealth ultimately preserved and multiplied over time.

The most common liquidity event is an acquisition.

In an acquisition, another company purchases the founder's business either partially or entirely. Acquisitions may occur through cash transactions, stock exchanges, earnout agreements, or hybrid structures combining multiple forms of compensation. Acquisitions are attractive because they often provide immediate liquidity and may eliminate much of the operational burden associated with scaling independently.

However, acquisitions also involve negotiation complexity.

The headline purchase price does not always reflect what founders ultimately receive personally. Financing structures, investor liquidation preferences, debt obligations, taxes, escrow holdbacks, performance milestones, employee retention agreements, and stock compensation terms can all affect final outcomes.

This is why sophisticated founders focus heavily on deal structure rather than only headline valuation numbers.

For example, a founder selling a company for two hundred million dollars may receive dramatically different personal outcomes depending on investor ownership percentages, liquidation terms, tax structures, and acquisition mechanics. In some situations, investors may receive large portions of proceeds before founders participate significantly due to preferred equity structures.

Understanding these dynamics before negotiating a sale is essential.

Another major liquidity pathway is the Initial Public Offering, or IPO.

An IPO allows private companies to sell shares to public market investors through stock exchanges. Public listings create liquidity opportunities because shares become tradable in open financial markets. IPOs also provide access to enormous pools of institutional capital and may significantly increase company valuation.

However, IPOs do not automatically create immediate founder liquidity.

Most founders face lock-up periods following IPOs. During these periods, insiders are restricted from selling shares for a specified amount of time, often six months or longer. This prevents sudden large insider selling that could destabilize public market confidence.

As a result, founders may become "paper billionaires" publicly while remaining temporarily unable to access much of their wealth immediately.

This creates psychological complexity.

Founders often experience intense emotional pressure during post-IPO periods because stock prices fluctuate daily under public scrutiny. Media narratives, analyst reports, quarterly earnings expectations, and market volatility suddenly become major influences on personal net worth.

Many founders are unprepared for this transition. Private entrepreneurship and public market leadership require different psychological skill sets. Founders must adapt from building privately to operating under constant institutional observation and shareholder expectations.

Another important liquidity structure involves direct listings.

Unlike traditional IPOs, direct listings allow companies to enter public markets without issuing new shares through underwriters. Existing shareholders may gain liquidity more directly because shares become tradable publicly without the same capital-raising structure used in traditional IPOs.

Direct listings may reduce underwriting costs and dilution while providing market-based price discovery. However, they are generally more appropriate for companies with strong brand recognition, existing investor demand, and healthy financial positioning.

SPAC mergers represent another alternative liquidity pathway.

A Special Purpose Acquisition Company, or SPAC, raises public market capital first and later merges with a private operating company. Through this process, private companies may enter public markets faster than through traditional IPO structures.

SPAC transactions became extremely popular during certain market cycles because they offered faster timelines, negotiated valuations, and greater certainty around pricing structures. However, many SPAC transactions also introduced volatility, regulatory scrutiny, and post-merger performance challenges.

Founders considering SPACs must evaluate whether long-term market readiness truly exists beyond the short-term attractiveness of accelerated liquidity.

Another important form of liquidity involves secondary transactions.

Secondary markets allow founders, employees, or early investors to sell portions of private company shares before traditional exits occur. These transactions may happen privately through institutional buyers, venture funds, or specialized secondary market platforms.

Secondary liquidity can dramatically affect founder psychology.

Entrepreneurs who remain fully illiquid for many years often experience emotional stress because their financial future depends entirely on uncertain future events. Partial secondary liquidity can provide financial stability without eliminating long-term upside participation.

For example, a founder may sell five percent of personal holdings during a late-stage financing round while retaining substantial ownership for future appreciation. This may allow the founder to diversify investments, support family members, purchase property, or reduce personal debt while continuing to benefit from future company growth.

This balance is extremely important.

Many founders make poor decisions because they feel trapped financially. When entrepreneurs lack personal liquidity entirely, fear and stress may influence strategic choices. Founders may reject good acquisition offers due to unrealistic expectations or accept poor offers due to financial exhaustion.

Partial liquidity can improve decision-making quality significantly.

Another major liquidity concept involves recapitalization.

In recapitalizations, investors or private equity firms restructure ownership and capital structures while allowing founders to monetize portions of equity. These transactions often occur in mature private companies that generate strong cash flow but are not necessarily pursuing immediate public offerings.

Recapitalizations can create founder liquidity while maintaining operational independence.

For example, a founder may sell a portion of ownership to private equity while continuing to operate the business as CEO. This creates immediate financial rewards while preserving future upside potential through remaining ownership stakes.

This hybrid structure has become increasingly popular because it allows founders to reduce risk without fully exiting.

One of the most overlooked aspects of liquidity events is taxes.

Taxes can dramatically affect realized founder wealth. Sophisticated founders understand that tax planning is not something addressed after a liquidity event occurs. It must be planned strategically long beforehand.

Capital gains taxes, state taxes, international tax exposure, stock option taxation, qualified small business stock rules, trust structures, charitable planning, and estate strategies can all affect final outcomes dramatically.

A founder who neglects tax planning may lose enormous amounts of wealth unnecessarily.

This is why elite founders build advisory teams including tax attorneys, accountants, estate planners, wealth managers, and corporate lawyers long before major exits occur.

Another critical area involves emotional readiness.

Liquidity events are not only financial transactions. They are deeply psychological experiences.

For years, many founders tie personal identity directly to company growth. The business represents sacrifice, ambition, creativity, stress, and personal meaning. When liquidity occurs through acquisitions or public offerings, founders often experience emotional confusion unexpectedly.

Some feel liberated.

Others feel lost.

Many founders struggle after exits because they spent years pursuing one singular mission without preparing emotionally for what comes afterward. Financial freedom does not automatically create fulfillment. In fact, some founders experience emptiness after major exits because the intense purpose that once structured daily life suddenly disappears.

This is why sophisticated founders think carefully about life after liquidity.

Some pursue philanthropy. Others launch new ventures. Some become investors or mentors. Others focus on family, travel, wellness, education, or passion projects. Long-term fulfillment often depends on building identity beyond the company itself.

Another important concept in liquidity management is timing. Market conditions heavily influence liquidity outcomes. Bull markets often create higher valuations, stronger investor demand, and more favorable deal structures. Economic downturns may reduce acquisition activity, compress valuations, and limit exit opportunities.

Sophisticated founders monitor market cycles carefully.

They understand that liquidity timing can affect wealth outcomes dramatically. Some founders intentionally accelerate exits during favorable markets. Others delay transactions when they believe future market conditions will improve.

Timing is rarely perfect, but awareness matters.

One of the most difficult founder decisions involves determining whether to hold or sell.

This decision often becomes emotionally complicated because entrepreneurs believe deeply in future company potential. Some founders reject acquisitions that later appear undervalued in hindsight. Others reject life-changing offers only to experience industry disruption, competitive pressure, or market collapse later.

No founder can predict the future perfectly.

This is why many sophisticated entrepreneurs approach liquidity incrementally rather than absolutely. They may sell portions gradually while retaining future upside participation. This reduces regret risk because founders participate in both present liquidity and future growth potential.

Diversification also becomes critical after liquidity events occur.

Many founders remain psychologically attached to concentrated ownership positions even after achieving enormous wealth. While concentration often creates wealth initially, diversification usually preserves it more effectively over long periods.

Public markets fluctuate. Industries evolve. Technology changes. Regulations shift. Competitive landscapes transform.

Founders who diversify intelligently after liquidity events often preserve multigenerational wealth more successfully than those who remain excessively concentrated in a single asset.

Liquidity events also create opportunities for leverage beyond personal wealth.

Successful exits often increase founder credibility dramatically. Investors become more willing to fund future ventures. Strategic partnerships become easier. Access to elite networks expands. Media visibility increases. Future opportunities compound.

This explains why many serial entrepreneurs build wealth progressively across multiple ventures.

Each liquidity event creates not only financial capital but also social capital, strategic capital, and experiential capital.

Another critical lesson founders eventually learn is that wealth preservation requires different skills than wealth creation.

Building a company requires aggressive execution, risk tolerance, resilience, innovation, and operational intensity. Preserving wealth often requires patience, diversification, risk management, tax efficiency, estate planning, and disciplined allocation strategies.

Many founders excel at creating wealth but struggle to preserve it.

Sophisticated entrepreneurs therefore surround themselves with experienced advisors who specialize in long-term capital preservation after liquidity events occur.

Ultimately, liquidity represents the bridge between ownership and usable wealth.

It transforms years of enterprise building into financial freedom, strategic flexibility, and future opportunity. But liquidity events must be approached intelligently. Poor planning can destroy wealth. Emotional decisions can create regret. Weak structures can reduce founder outcomes dramatically.

The founders who build lasting wealth are often those who prepare for liquidity long before it arrives.

They understand ownership structures, taxes, market timing, diversification, negotiation dynamics, emotional psychology, and long-term capital preservation strategies. They recognize that creating value is only the first half of the journey.

Converting that value into enduring wealth is the second half.

And mastering both is what separates successful entrepreneurs from truly wealthy founders.

The Exit That Changed Everything

Ethan Walker sat alone in the conference room overlooking San Francisco Bay while lawyers finalized the acquisition documents on the other side of the glass wall. The city lights reflected against the dark water outside, but Ethan barely noticed them anymore. His attention remained fixed on the thick stack of papers sitting silently in front of him.

After eleven years of building his artificial intelligence company, the moment had finally arrived. By the next morning, he would officially become one of the youngest tech founders in the country to complete a multi-billion-dollar acquisition.

Yet instead of excitement, Ethan felt strangely numb.

For years he imagined this exact moment. He pictured celebration, relief, and emotional victory. He thought financial freedom would feel overwhelming and euphoric. But now that the deal was real, his emotions felt far more complicated.

The company had started with almost nothing.

At twenty-six years old, Ethan had left a stable engineering career after becoming obsessed with predictive AI systems for logistics optimization. His friends thought he was making a reckless mistake. Investors rejected him repeatedly during the first year. Potential customers dismissed the product as unrealistic. At one point, Ethan maxed out personal credit cards simply to keep servers operating.

There were months when payroll barely cleared.

Months when he questioned his own sanity.

Months when failure felt inevitable.

But over time, the technology improved. Early customers renewed contracts. Revenue stabilized. Then a major retail distribution company adopted the platform nationally, reducing operational costs dramatically across its network.

Everything accelerated after that.

Investors suddenly became interested. Venture capital firms competed aggressively to fund expansion. Within five years, the company transformed from a struggling startup into one of the fastest-growing AI infrastructure businesses in the industry.

The valuation skyrocketed.

Financial media praised Ethan constantly. Industry analysts called him visionary. Young entrepreneurs flooded his inbox asking for advice. Public attention grew rapidly, but few people understood how emotionally exhausting the journey had actually become.

Despite the massive valuation headlines, Ethan still lived relatively modestly compared to what outsiders imagined. Most of his wealth remained locked inside private company shares. On paper, he looked enormously wealthy. In reality, much of that wealth was inaccessible.

He often joked privately that he was "rich but trapped."

Everything changed when global technology companies began approaching him about acquisition possibilities.

The offers arrived slowly at first.

Then aggressively.

One multinational corporation eventually proposed a deal so large that Ethan initially thought the numbers were a mistake. The acquisition would create enough personal wealth not only for him, but for generations of his family.

Still, he hesitated.

The company represented far more than money to him. It represented identity. Purpose. Sacrifice. Every office move, every product launch, every failed version, every all-night coding session, every difficult hiring decision, every investor negotiation—all of it was emotionally embedded into the business itself.

Selling felt strangely personal.

During negotiations, Ethan became obsessed with one question:

"What happens after this?"

Nobody seemed prepared to answer it honestly.

Bankers discussed valuation. Lawyers discussed contracts. Investors discussed returns. Tax advisors discussed structures. But very few people talked about the psychological side of liquidity. Late one evening, Ethan met privately with an older founder named Marcus Levin, who had sold a cybersecurity company years earlier. Marcus listened quietly while Ethan described his anxiety surrounding the acquisition.

Finally, Marcus leaned back in his chair and said something Ethan never forgot.

"You think this deal is about money. It's actually about identity."

The words unsettled him.

Marcus explained that many founders unconsciously build their entire emotional structure around company growth. The mission becomes addictive. The pressure becomes familiar. The struggle creates meaning. When liquidity finally arrives, many founders discover that financial freedom solves external problems but not internal purpose.

Ethan thought about those words constantly afterward.

As negotiations continued, he realized he was not actually afraid of selling the company. He was afraid of losing the version of himself that existed inside the company.

That realization changed how he approached the deal entirely.

Instead of focusing purely on valuation, Ethan began thinking more carefully about life after liquidity. He structured long-term investment plans. He discussed philanthropy goals with advisors. He explored opportunities to mentor younger founders and invest in emerging technologies.

Most importantly, he stopped viewing the acquisition as an ending.

He started viewing it as a transition.

The deal closed nine months later.

Financial media exploded with coverage overnight. Articles called Ethan a billionaire founder. Social media praised the acquisition as one of the most successful AI exits of the decade. Former classmates suddenly reached out after years of silence.

But privately, Ethan's first emotion was not excitement.

It was relief.

For the first time in over a decade, survival pressure disappeared completely. The years of uncertainty, financial stress, and emotional exhaustion finally lifted.

Then something unexpected happened.

Two months after the acquisition, Ethan became deeply restless. Without the company consuming every waking hour, he struggled emotionally. His schedule felt empty. The intensity that once structured daily life vanished almost overnight. He traveled, relaxed, bought properties, and invested capital, yet none of it recreated the sense of purpose he once felt while building the company.

Marcus had been right.

Liquidity changed finances instantly, but identity evolved more slowly.

Eventually, Ethan realized something important.

The greatest reward from entrepreneurship was never purely the money itself.

It was the ability to create.

The ability to build systems, solve problems, lead people, and shape the future through ideas.

Once he understood this, everything changed again.

Instead of retiring permanently, Ethan began investing in young founders. He helped entrepreneurs avoid mistakes he once made himself. He funded educational initiatives for engineers from low-income backgrounds. He launched a small innovation fund supporting early-stage AI infrastructure startups.

Ironically, after liquidity removed financial pressure entirely, Ethan became more creative than ever before.

He no longer built companies for survival.

He built them for impact.

Years later, during a private founder conference, a young entrepreneur nervously asked Ethan whether selling his company had been worth it.

Ethan paused for a long moment before answering.

“The money changes your lifestyle,” he said quietly. “But the real lesson is learning who you are when survival is no longer your motivation.”

The room fell silent.

Then Ethan smiled slightly before adding one final sentence that summarized everything he had learned about founder wealth.

"Liquidity gives you freedom. What you do with that freedom determines whether you actually become wealthy."

Chapter 4

Building Enterprise Value That Attracts Major Investors and Buyers

One of the most important truths in founder wealth creation is that liquidity events rarely happen by accident. Major acquisitions, institutional investments, public offerings, and large-scale exits usually occur because founders intentionally build companies that attract capital. Investors and buyers are constantly searching for scalable, defensible, profitable, and strategically positioned businesses capable of generating long-term returns. Founders who understand how enterprise value is created place themselves in a dramatically stronger position to build wealth through future equity events.

Enterprise value represents far more than revenue alone.

Many entrepreneurs mistakenly assume that generating sales automatically creates a valuable company. While revenue is important, sophisticated investors evaluate businesses using a much broader framework. They analyze scalability, margins, recurring revenue, operational efficiency, leadership quality, intellectual property, market positioning, customer retention, competitive advantages, growth velocity, and long-term expansion potential. The companies that command the highest valuations are often not simply the companies earning the most money today. They are the companies investors believe can dominate markets tomorrow.

This distinction changes how founders build businesses.

Instead of focusing purely on short-term profitability, sophisticated entrepreneurs begin optimizing for enterprise attractiveness. They understand that buyers and investors are evaluating not only current financial performance but also future potential, risk reduction, scalability, and strategic leverage.

One of the first drivers of enterprise value is recurring revenue.

Recurring revenue businesses are highly attractive because they create predictability. Investors value predictability because predictable cash flow reduces uncertainty and improves future financial forecasting. Subscription-based software companies, membership businesses, recurring service contracts, SaaS platforms, licensing models, and subscription media businesses often command significantly higher valuation multiples than businesses dependent on inconsistent transactional sales.

For example, a company generating ten million dollars annually through predictable recurring subscriptions may receive a much higher valuation than a company generating the same revenue through one-time transactions. Investors understand that recurring customers often indicate stronger retention, scalable systems, and more stable long-term growth.

This is why many modern founders aggressively transition toward recurring business models whenever possible.

Predictability increases valuation.

Another major driver of enterprise value is scalability.

Scalable businesses can increase revenue dramatically without proportionally increasing costs. This creates operating leverage. Investors love operating leverage because it allows profit margins to expand as the company grows.

Technology businesses frequently attract high valuations because software can often scale globally with relatively low incremental distribution costs. Once the product infrastructure is built, adding additional users may require minimal additional expense compared to traditional labor-intensive businesses.

However, scalability is not limited to technology companies.

Education businesses, media brands, licensing businesses, franchising systems, financial platforms, digital marketplaces, online course ecosystems, and automated service infrastructures can also scale effectively when structured properly.

Founders who build scalable systems rather than founder-dependent operations create far greater enterprise value over time.

This requires operational discipline.

Many small business owners unintentionally limit valuation because the company depends too heavily on the founder personally. If the founder handles all sales, operations, client relationships, decision-making, and strategic direction alone, investors perceive higher risk. A business heavily dependent on one person is less transferable and therefore less valuable.

Sophisticated founders solve this problem by building systems.

They create documented processes, management teams, operational frameworks, technology infrastructure, automation systems, reporting structures, and repeatable workflows that allow the company to function independently of the founder's daily involvement.

This increases enterprise value significantly because buyers and investors prefer businesses that can continue scaling without relying entirely on a single individual. Another critical factor is market size. Investors seek companies operating within large or rapidly expanding markets because large markets create room for future growth. Even highly profitable businesses may receive lower valuations if market expansion opportunities appear limited.

This is why founders must understand total addressable market dynamics.

A company dominating a tiny niche may eventually reach growth limitations, while a company capturing even a small percentage of a massive global market may have extraordinary long-term upside potential.

Investors often ask one central question:

"How large can this company realistically become?"

The answer heavily influences valuation.

This is also why visionary storytelling matters in entrepreneurship.

Sophisticated founders learn how to communicate not only what the company currently is, but what it could become. They present scalable visions supported by operational execution, market trends, customer demand, and long-term strategic positioning.

Storytelling without execution creates hype. Execution without vision creates limitation.

The highest-value companies combine both.

Another essential component of enterprise value is customer retention.

Acquiring customers is important, but retaining customers is often far more valuable. Businesses with strong retention rates indicate product quality, customer satisfaction, operational consistency, and sustainable long-term revenue potential.

High customer churn creates concern because investors worry future growth may be unstable or expensive to maintain. Strong retention, however, suggests durability and customer loyalty.

This is especially important in subscription-based businesses.

Founders who focus only on aggressive acquisition while ignoring retention often build fragile companies. Sustainable enterprise value requires balancing growth with long-term customer satisfaction and loyalty.

Margins also play a major role in valuation.

Businesses with healthy gross margins and strong operating margins generally attract more investor interest because higher margins provide flexibility during economic downturns, expansion phases, and competitive pressure. Many founders mistakenly chase growth at all costs without understanding profitability dynamics. While certain high-growth companies may temporarily prioritize expansion over profits, long-term enterprise value ultimately depends on the company's ability to generate sustainable economic returns.

Investors want evidence that growth can eventually produce durable profitability.

This becomes especially important in public markets where institutional investors analyze financial efficiency closely.

Another major enterprise value driver is intellectual property.

Patents, proprietary technology, trademarks, unique systems, exclusive data, brand equity, algorithms, distribution networks, and operational processes can create competitive barriers that increase valuation significantly.

Businesses with strong defensibility are more attractive because competitors cannot easily replicate them.

For example, a company with proprietary AI infrastructure, patented biotechnology, exclusive licensing rights, or dominant platform network effects may command extraordinary valuations because investors believe future competition will struggle to disrupt market leadership.

Brand equity itself can become enormously valuable.

Some companies achieve premium valuations because customers trust the brand deeply. Brand trust creates pricing power, customer loyalty, lower acquisition costs, and market influence.

This is why sophisticated founders invest heavily in reputation, consistency, customer experience, and long-term brand positioning.

Strong brands compound value over time.

Leadership quality also affects enterprise valuation significantly.

Investors evaluate founders carefully because leadership execution heavily influences future performance. A strong leadership team increases investor confidence while weak or unstable leadership creates risk.

Founders who attract elite executives, advisors, operational leaders, and board members often strengthen enterprise value dramatically because institutional investors view strong teams as indicators of scalability and governance maturity.

This is why founder evolution matters.

The skills required to launch a startup are different from the skills required to scale a large enterprise. Some founders struggle during scaling phases because they resist delegation, avoid structure, or fail to evolve operationally.

Sophisticated founders adapt continuously.

They develop leadership maturity, financial understanding, strategic communication skills, hiring discipline, and operational sophistication as the company grows.

Another essential component of enterprise value is financial reporting quality.

Institutional investors and acquirers require transparency. Clean financial statements, organized reporting systems, audited records, compliance structures, legal clarity, and operational visibility all increase investor confidence.

Messy accounting, unclear ownership structures, inconsistent reporting, unresolved legal risks, or poor compliance systems reduce valuation because buyers perceive operational danger.

Founders who prepare early for institutional scrutiny gain major advantages later.

This is one reason sophisticated entrepreneurs often build professional infrastructure long before pursuing major exits.

Another important factor is growth consistency. Extreme volatility creates investor concern. While fast growth is attractive, sustainable growth with operational discipline often commands stronger long-term confidence than chaotic expansion unsupported by systems.

Investors want evidence that the company can continue executing predictably at larger scales.

This becomes especially important as companies approach IPO readiness or institutional acquisition discussions.

Another major driver of enterprise value is strategic positioning.

Some companies become highly valuable because they solve critical industry problems or occupy strategically important positions within broader ecosystems. A business may become attractive not only because of standalone profits but because larger corporations view it as strategically essential.

For example, a cybersecurity platform protecting enterprise infrastructure may become highly attractive to large technology firms seeking competitive advantages. A logistics platform with valuable transportation data may become strategically important to global retailers. An AI platform with proprietary healthcare analytics may become highly valuable to pharmaceutical companies.

Strategic value often creates acquisition premiums.

Founders who understand industry dynamics can intentionally position companies to become highly attractive acquisition targets.

Network effects also create extraordinary enterprise value.

A network effect occurs when a product or platform becomes more valuable as more users join. Social media platforms, marketplaces, financial exchanges, communication systems, and software ecosystems often benefit from network effects because scale itself strengthens competitive advantage.

Businesses with strong network effects often achieve dominant market positions and exceptionally high valuations because competitors struggle to replicate user ecosystems once scale becomes established.

Another critical element is timing.

Market conditions influence valuation significantly. Certain industries experience periods of intense investor enthusiasm driven by technological trends, economic shifts, consumer behavior changes, or regulatory developments.

Artificial intelligence, cybersecurity, fintech, biotechnology, renewable energy, automation, and digital infrastructure have all experienced major valuation expansions during specific market cycles.

Sophisticated founders understand how macroeconomic trends affect investor appetite.

They position businesses strategically within emerging opportunities while building operational substance behind market narratives.

However, founders must avoid becoming dependent solely on hype cycles.

Temporary market excitement without sustainable fundamentals often leads to valuation collapses later.

True enterprise value requires both narrative strength and operational execution.

Another overlooked factor in building enterprise value is optionality.

Companies with multiple future pathways often receive stronger valuations because investors perceive flexibility. A business capable of pursuing acquisitions, IPOs, strategic partnerships, licensing expansion, international growth, or private equity recapitalization creates multiple future liquidity possibilities.

Optionality reduces investor risk. The more strategic pathways available, the more attractive the company becomes.

This is why sophisticated founders rarely build companies with only one possible outcome in mind. They create strategic flexibility that allows adaptation as markets evolve.

Ultimately, enterprise value is not built through luck.

It is engineered intentionally through operational systems, financial discipline, scalability, market positioning, leadership quality, customer retention, strategic branding, intellectual property, and long-term execution.

Founders who understand these principles stop building businesses merely to survive.

They begin building assets designed to attract capital, command premium valuations, create strategic leverage, and generate long-term wealth through future equity events.

This transformation changes how entrepreneurs think, operate, hire, market, expand, and scale.

Because once a founder understands what sophisticated investors and buyers truly value, they begin building companies very differently.

And that difference often determines whether a business remains small—or becomes a wealth-generating enterprise capable of changing generations.

The Company Nobody Wanted—Until Everyone Did

When Olivia Chen launched her digital healthcare platform from a tiny shared workspace in Austin, almost nobody believed the business would survive.

Investors dismissed the idea repeatedly.

Most venture capital firms argued that the healthcare industry moved too slowly for scalable technology adoption. Others claimed regulatory barriers would make expansion nearly impossible. Some investors openly told Olivia that healthcare startups were too complicated, too expensive, and too risky compared to consumer technology businesses.

But Olivia saw something others missed.

She believed healthcare providers desperately needed better systems to automate patient scheduling, insurance verification, digital records integration, and preventative care communication. More importantly, she believed the future of healthcare would depend heavily on scalable digital infrastructure.

For nearly two years, almost no one cared.

The company struggled constantly. Revenue remained inconsistent. Product development costs were high. Healthcare providers moved cautiously. Investors showed little enthusiasm. Olivia personally handled customer onboarding, support calls, sales meetings, hiring, and product testing while sleeping only a few hours most nights.

Many founders would have quit.

But Olivia became obsessed with one idea: building enterprise value instead of chasing quick attention.

She noticed that many startups focused heavily on marketing hype while neglecting operational strength. Olivia decided her company would become different. If investors were not interested yet, she would build a business impossible to ignore later.

So she focused relentlessly on fundamentals.

The company improved customer retention obsessively. Every healthcare provider received personal onboarding support. The engineering team refined automation systems continuously. Olivia invested heavily in product reliability even when growth slowed temporarily.

Most importantly, she built recurring revenue.

Instead of relying on one-time implementation fees, Olivia structured the platform around subscription contracts. Each new clinic generated monthly recurring revenue that compounded predictably over time.

At first, growth felt painfully slow.

But gradually, something powerful began happening.

Customer churn dropped dramatically. Existing clinics expanded contracts voluntarily. Referrals increased organically because healthcare providers trusted the system.

The company became deeply integrated into client operations, making the software difficult to replace.

That changed everything.

One afternoon, Olivia received an unexpected call from a mid-sized healthcare investment fund requesting a meeting. Unlike previous investors, this group focused heavily on recurring revenue metrics, retention rates, operational scalability, and infrastructure durability.

They immediately recognized what Olivia had built.

The business was no longer just software.

It was becoming healthcare infrastructure.

The investment fund offered capital, but Olivia approached negotiations differently now. Years earlier, she would have accepted almost any deal out of desperation. Instead, she carefully evaluated valuation, ownership impact, governance terms, and long-term strategic alignment.

She had learned that enterprise value was not only about receiving investment.

It was about building leverage before negotiating.

The deal closed successfully, allowing the company to expand engineering, improve compliance systems, and accelerate customer acquisition nationally.

Growth exploded over the next four years.

The platform expanded into hospitals, insurance groups, telemedicine systems, and national healthcare networks. Revenue scaled rapidly because the infrastructure itself was highly scalable. Adding new customers required relatively low incremental costs compared to the growing recurring revenue base.

Then the acquisition interest started.

Major technology firms approached quietly at first. Then larger healthcare conglomerates entered discussions. Investment banks called regularly. Industry analysts began describing Olivia's company as a "strategic healthcare infrastructure asset."

Olivia noticed something fascinating during negotiations.

The buyers rarely focused only on current revenue.

Instead, they talked constantly about future market dominance, customer integration depth, recurring revenue durability, data infrastructure, and strategic positioning within healthcare ecosystems.

They were evaluating enterprise value.

One global healthcare corporation eventually offered an acquisition price far beyond anything Olivia imagined during the company's early years.

During final negotiations, one executive explained exactly why the company had become so valuable.

"You didn't build an app," he told her. "You built infrastructure that healthcare providers depend on daily. That creates enormous long-term strategic value."

The sentence stayed with Olivia forever.

Years earlier, investors ignored the company because they focused only on short-term excitement. Olivia succeeded because she focused on long-term enterprise strength.

After the acquisition closed, financial media praised Olivia as an overnight success story. Headlines celebrated the billion-dollar exit. Podcasts invited her to discuss entrepreneurship and founder wealth.

But privately, Olivia knew the truth.

The company became valuable long before the acquisition happened.

Its value was built slowly through retention, scalability, recurring revenue, operational systems, customer trust, infrastructure depth, and strategic positioning.

Most people saw the liquidity event.

Very few understood the years of intentional enterprise building that made the liquidity event possible in the first place.

Later, during a founder mentorship event, a young entrepreneur asked Olivia what investors truly wanted.

Olivia smiled quietly before answering.

"Investors don't just buy revenue," she said. "They buy confidence in the future."

The audience listened carefully. Then Olivia added the lesson that defined her entire journey.

"If you build a company people depend on, eventually investors and buyers will compete to own part of it."

Chapter 5

Venture Capital, Private Equity, and Institutional Money: Understanding the Capital Behind Massive Founder Wealth

One of the defining characteristics of modern wealth creation is the relationship between founders and institutional capital. While many entrepreneurs begin companies independently, large-scale growth often requires access to significant financial resources. Venture capital firms, private equity groups, institutional investors, family offices, sovereign wealth funds, hedge funds, and strategic corporate investors all play major roles in shaping the modern business landscape.

Founders who understand how institutional money works gain a powerful advantage.

Institutional capital is not simply about receiving money. It is about understanding how capital markets think, how investors evaluate opportunities, how financing structures affect ownership, and how strategic partnerships can accelerate enterprise value dramatically. Many of the world's largest founder fortunes were created not only through innovation and operational execution, but through intelligently leveraging external capital to scale faster than would have been possible independently.

However, institutional money also introduces complexity.

External investors bring expectations, governance structures, performance pressure, reporting requirements, strategic influence, and ownership dilution. Founders who fail to understand these dynamics may lose control, reduce long-term wealth, or damage company culture unintentionally. Founders who master these relationships, however, can transform relatively small startups into global enterprises capable of generating enormous equity value.

Understanding institutional capital begins with understanding incentives.

Investors are not charities. They allocate capital expecting future returns. Venture capital firms seek companies capable of extraordinary growth because they understand most startups fail. A single successful investment may need to generate returns large enough to offset numerous unsuccessful investments within the portfolio.

This risk-reward dynamic explains why venture capital firms aggressively pursue scalability.

Venture investors often prioritize companies capable of becoming category leaders, dominant platforms, or billion-dollar enterprises. They seek asymmetric upside opportunities where a relatively small investment could eventually produce massive returns.

As a result, venture-backed companies are often encouraged to grow aggressively.

Speed becomes important.

Market share becomes important.

Scalability becomes important.

This creates both opportunity and pressure for founders.

In the earliest stages of institutional fundraising, founders often pursue seed capital. Seed investors may include angel investors, early-stage venture funds, successful entrepreneurs, family offices, or specialized startup investors willing to take significant risks on unproven companies.

At this stage, investors often evaluate founders more heavily than financial performance because operating history may still be limited.

Investors analyze vision, leadership quality, adaptability, market understanding, resilience, technical expertise, communication ability, and execution potential. A founder's ability to inspire confidence can significantly influence early fundraising success.

This is why storytelling becomes a critical entrepreneurial skill.

Sophisticated founders learn how to communicate large visions supported by realistic execution strategies. They present not only current traction but also future opportunity. They explain how the company could scale, dominate markets, create defensibility, and generate extraordinary returns over time.

The best founders combine optimism with operational credibility.

After seed financing, companies often progress toward larger institutional rounds such as Series A, Series B, Series C, and growth-stage financing. At each stage, investor expectations evolve.

Early investors may tolerate experimentation and uncertainty. Later-stage institutional investors generally demand stronger operational metrics, financial discipline, governance systems, and scalable infrastructure.

As companies mature, investors increasingly focus on measurable indicators such as revenue growth, customer acquisition efficiency, retention rates, gross margins, operating leverage, profitability pathways, and market positioning. This evolution forces founders to grow as leaders.

The founder capable of launching a startup may not automatically possess the skills required to lead a multi-billion-dollar enterprise. Sophisticated founders recognize this and intentionally evolve operationally, strategically, and psychologically throughout each stage of growth.

One of the most important distinctions founders must understand is the difference between venture capital and private equity.

Although both involve institutional investment, their strategies often differ significantly.

Venture capital firms typically invest in earlier-stage, high-growth companies with substantial future upside potential. These businesses may still be unprofitable but capable of scaling rapidly if growth succeeds.

Private equity firms, on the other hand, often invest in more mature companies with stable cash flow, operational infrastructure, and established market presence. Private equity investors frequently focus on operational optimization, profitability improvement, acquisitions, recapitalizations, and financial engineering.

This distinction affects founder relationships with investors.

Venture investors often emphasize growth acceleration.

Private equity investors often emphasize operational efficiency and financial performance.

Founders must understand which type of capital aligns best with company objectives and long-term vision.

Not all capital is equal.

Many inexperienced entrepreneurs assume any investment is positive. Sophisticated founders understand that investor alignment matters tremendously. The wrong investors may create destructive pressure, misaligned incentives, toxic governance conflicts, or strategic instability.

This is why founder-investor relationships should be approached like long-term partnerships rather than simple financial transactions.

A strong investor may provide far more than money alone.

Exceptional investors can offer strategic guidance, industry introductions, acquisition pathways, executive recruitment support, operational expertise, customer relationships, media credibility, future fundraising access, and long-term mentorship.

Some investors become transformative strategic allies.

Others become distractions or obstacles.

Choosing investors carefully is therefore one of the most important founder decisions.

Another critical concept is board governance.

As institutional investors enter companies, they often receive board seats or governance influence. Boards play major roles in strategic oversight, executive decisions, financing approvals, acquisitions, compensation structures, and long-term direction.

Strong boards can dramatically strengthen companies.

Weak boards can create instability.

Sophisticated founders learn how to build balanced boards containing operational expertise, financial understanding, industry relationships, and long-term strategic perspective. They also learn how to manage board dynamics professionally while preserving leadership authority appropriately.

Governance becomes increasingly important as companies approach large-scale liquidity events.

Institutional investors also influence company culture significantly.

Growth-stage companies frequently experience rapid hiring, operational expansion, and organizational complexity after major fundraising rounds. Founders who fail to protect cultural integrity during hypergrowth often experience internal dysfunction, communication breakdowns, and leadership instability.

This is one reason some founders intentionally raise capital more slowly.

They understand that excessive growth without operational readiness can damage long-term value.

The relationship between capital and growth must remain balanced.

Another major institutional financing concept involves valuation inflation.

During favorable market cycles, companies may receive extremely high valuations due to investor enthusiasm. While high valuations may appear attractive initially, they can create dangerous expectations later.

A company raising money at an excessively inflated valuation may struggle during future financing rounds if growth fails to justify previous pricing. This may lead to down rounds where new financing occurs at lower valuations than previous rounds.

Down rounds can severely damage morale, investor confidence, employee equity value, and founder reputation.

Sophisticated founders therefore think carefully about sustainable valuation growth rather than chasing vanity numbers.

Long-term credibility matters more than temporary hype.

Institutional investors also pay close attention to unit economics.

Many startups prioritize aggressive growth while neglecting profitability fundamentals. However, sustainable enterprise value ultimately depends on whether companies can generate attractive long-term economic returns.

Customer acquisition cost, lifetime customer value, retention rates, margins, operational efficiency, and scalability all become increasingly important as companies mature.

Founders who understand financial mechanics gain major advantages during investor negotiations.

Another important concept is capital efficiency.

Some companies require enormous capital simply to operate. Others achieve strong growth using relatively modest resources. Capital-efficient businesses often gain strategic flexibility because they are less dependent on continuous fundraising.

During economic downturns, this flexibility becomes critical.

Companies overly dependent on investor capital may struggle when funding markets tighten. Businesses with strong operational discipline and healthy cash management often survive difficult environments more effectively.

This explains why sophisticated founders focus heavily on runway management.

Runway refers to how long a company can operate before requiring additional financing. Maintaining healthy runway allows founders to negotiate from positions of strength rather than desperation.

Desperation weakens leverage.

Leverage affects ownership outcomes.

Ownership outcomes affect long-term founder wealth.

Another major aspect of institutional money involves exit expectations.

Most institutional investors eventually seek liquidity events. Venture capital firms typically operate using fund structures with defined timelines. They invest expecting eventual exits through IPOs, acquisitions, or secondary transactions. This means founder goals and investor timelines must remain aligned.

Conflicts often emerge when founders want to maintain independence while investors seek exits. Sophisticated founders discuss long-term objectives openly with investors early in relationships to minimize future friction.

Institutional capital also affects founder psychology.

After raising substantial investment, founders often experience increased pressure because external expectations intensify. Media scrutiny may increase. Employee count grows rapidly. Burn rates rise. Investors expect measurable progress.

Some founders thrive under this pressure.

Others become emotionally overwhelmed.

This is why emotional resilience becomes critical during high-growth stages.

Founders must learn how to manage uncertainty, investor communication, public perception, internal leadership challenges, and operational volatility simultaneously.

Another important institutional concept is strategic capital. Some investors provide more than financial resources because they operate strategically within industries. Large corporations may invest in startups to gain technological access, market intelligence, acquisition options, or ecosystem positioning.

Strategic investors can accelerate growth dramatically when alignment exists.

However, strategic capital also introduces complexity because investor motivations may extend beyond financial returns alone.

Founders must evaluate these relationships carefully.

Another increasingly important source of institutional money involves sovereign wealth funds and global capital pools.

Large international investors now allocate enormous amounts of capital into technology, infrastructure, AI, healthcare, fintech, renewable energy, and digital platforms globally. Founders building scalable businesses may eventually interact with capital sources operating across multiple continents.

Global capital flows influence valuation trends, competitive landscapes, and acquisition dynamics significantly.

Understanding macroeconomic trends therefore becomes increasingly important for sophisticated founders. Interest rates, monetary policy, market liquidity, geopolitical stability, technological shifts, and economic cycles all influence investor behavior.

During low-interest-rate environments, institutional investors often pursue higher-risk growth assets aggressively. During tighter monetary periods, investors may prioritize profitability and operational discipline more heavily.

Founders who understand these cycles position companies more intelligently.

One of the most important long-term lessons about institutional capital is this:

Capital amplifies.

If the underlying business model is strong, institutional money may accelerate extraordinary growth.

If the underlying business lacks operational substance, institutional money may simply accelerate failure.

Money alone does not create great companies.

Execution creates great companies.

Institutional capital magnifies execution quality.

Sophisticated founders therefore focus first on building operational excellence, market demand, scalable systems, strong leadership, and customer value. Then they use institutional capital strategically to expand faster and larger than would otherwise be possible.

Ultimately, understanding institutional money is essential because modern founder wealth creation rarely occurs in isolation. Capital markets shape valuations, growth opportunities, liquidity pathways, and strategic expansion possibilities.

Founders who understand how institutional investors think gain enormous strategic leverage.

They negotiate better.

They structure ownership more intelligently.

They preserve wealth more effectively.

They scale more strategically.

And most importantly, they build companies capable of attracting the kind of capital that transforms startups into global wealth-generating enterprises.

Because in the modern economy, some of the largest founder fortunes were not built simply through hard work alone. They were built through understanding how to combine vision, execution, ownership, and institutional capital into scalable engines of long-term value creation.

The Investor Meeting That Changed Maya's Future

Maya Thompson sat quietly in the waiting room of one of the largest venture capital firms in New York City, trying to control the nervous energy building inside her chest.

Outside the massive glass windows, Manhattan moved with its usual intensity. Yellow taxis flooded the streets below while thousands of people rushed between meetings, offices, restaurants, and skyscrapers filled with money, ambition, and competition.

Three years earlier, Maya had been working alone from a tiny apartment in Atlanta, trying desperately to build her online financial education platform for underserved communities. At the time, almost nobody took her seriously.

Now she was preparing to pitch institutional investors managing billions of dollars.

The journey to that moment had been brutal.

When Maya launched the company, she believed millions of people needed simpler financial education tools combined with AI-driven budgeting systems and personalized wealth-building guidance. But early growth came painfully slowly. Investors rejected her repeatedly, often claiming the market was too crowded or the target audience lacked profitability potential.

Several investors dismissed her idea within minutes.

One investor even told her directly that "financial literacy businesses don't scale."

The comment haunted her for months.

Still, Maya kept building.

Instead of obsessing over fundraising immediately, she focused on users. She studied customer behavior obsessively, improved retention, simplified onboarding, and refined the platform's subscription model until recurring revenue slowly began stabilizing.

That decision changed everything.

By the second year, the company reached profitability on a small scale. Customers remained loyal because the platform genuinely improved their financial behavior. Retention rates climbed steadily. Word-of-mouth referrals increased organically.

Most importantly, recurring monthly revenue compounded consistently.

Maya became obsessed with operational discipline.

While other startups burned enormous amounts of investor cash chasing headlines, she focused on unit economics, customer lifetime value, and sustainable growth systems. She hired slowly, documented processes carefully, and avoided unnecessary expenses.

At first, this conservative approach made the company look less exciting than heavily funded competitors.

But then the market shifted.

Rising interest rates and tighter funding conditions suddenly punished companies dependent on endless investor cash. Many highly publicized startups collapsed because their business models lacked operational sustainability.

Maya's company survived because it was built differently.

That survival created opportunity.

Institutional investors who once ignored her suddenly became interested because her company demonstrated something increasingly rare: scalable growth with strong financial discipline.

The invitation to New York came shortly afterward. As Maya waited nervously for the meeting to begin, she reviewed her notes repeatedly. She had practiced the presentation dozens of times. Still, part of her feared the same dismissive reactions she experienced years earlier.

Then the conference room doors opened.

Five investors entered calmly, carrying laptops and notebooks. The lead partner introduced himself politely before inviting Maya to begin.

For the first few minutes, Maya followed her prepared slides carefully. She explained customer growth, recurring revenue trends, retention rates, and operational systems.

Then something unexpected happened.

The investors stopped interrupting.

Instead of challenging her aggressively, they leaned forward and asked deeper strategic questions. They wanted to understand scalability, long-term margins, international expansion potential, and infrastructure capabilities.

For the first time, Maya realized they were no longer evaluating whether the company could survive.

They were evaluating how large it could become.

That realization changed her confidence instantly.

She stopped pitching from a place of desperation and started speaking from a place of strategic clarity. She explained how the platform could evolve into a complete financial ecosystem including education, budgeting, AI-driven wealth planning, lending partnerships, and financial automation tools.

The room became intensely focused.

One investor finally asked the question Maya had secretly hoped to hear for years.

"How big do you think this company can become?"

Without hesitation, Maya answered confidently.

"I think this can become the financial operating system for millions of families who've been ignored by traditional institutions."

Silence filled the room briefly.

Then the lead partner smiled slightly.

"That's a much larger vision than financial education," he said.

Maya nodded.

"Exactly."

The meeting lasted nearly three hours.

When Maya finally left the office, she felt emotionally exhausted but strangely calm. Regardless of the outcome, something important had shifted internally.

For years she viewed investors as gatekeepers controlling her future.

Now she understood something deeper.

Institutional capital was not about begging for approval.

It was about demonstrating enterprise value.

Two weeks later, the venture capital firm offered a major investment round at a valuation far beyond what Maya once believed possible.

But this time, she negotiated differently.

Earlier in her entrepreneurial journey, Maya would have accepted almost any terms out of fear. Now she understood ownership structures, dilution impact, governance rights, and long-term wealth preservation.

She negotiated carefully.

She selected board members strategically.

She protected operational flexibility.

Most importantly, she ensured investor alignment with the company's long-term mission rather than short-term hype.

The investment transformed the business.

The company expanded nationally, improved technology infrastructure, hired world-class engineers, and scaled marketing intelligently. Revenue accelerated dramatically over the following years.

But the biggest transformation happened inside Maya herself.

She no longer feared institutional money.

She understood it.

She realized investors were not searching for perfect founders or perfect companies. They were searching for scalable opportunities capable of generating extraordinary long-term value.

And she finally understood the real secret behind institutional capital:

Investors do not create great businesses.

They amplify great businesses that already possess strong fundamentals, leadership, and scalability. Years later, after her company eventually reached public markets, Maya often mentored younger entrepreneurs struggling with fundraising fear.

Many founders asked how to impress investors.

Maya always gave the same answer.

"Stop trying to impress investors," she said. "Focus on building something so valuable that capital naturally becomes attracted to it."

Then she would smile before adding the lesson she learned inside that Manhattan conference room years earlier.

"Money follows confidence. But institutional money follows enterprise value."

Chapter 6

IPO Psychology, Public Markets, and the Transformation From Founder to Public Company Leader

For many entrepreneurs, taking a company public represents the ultimate symbol of business success. An Initial Public Offering, or IPO, often signifies that a company has achieved enough scale, financial maturity, operational infrastructure, and market confidence to access global capital markets. IPOs can create extraordinary founder wealth, elevate company visibility, provide liquidity for investors and employees, and position businesses for massive future expansion.

Yet the transition from private founder to public company leader is one of the most psychologically demanding transformations in entrepreneurship.

Building a private company and operating a public company are fundamentally different experiences.

In private markets, founders often operate with significant flexibility. They may prioritize long-term experimentation, move quickly without excessive disclosure requirements, and maintain relative privacy regarding operational decisions and financial performance. Public markets, however, introduce a completely different environment defined by transparency, institutional scrutiny, regulatory obligations, quarterly reporting pressure, analyst expectations, and daily market reactions.

Many founders underestimate how dramatically this transition affects leadership psychology.

Going public changes not only how a company operates but also how founders think, communicate, lead, and emotionally process success and failure.

One of the first major changes involves visibility.

Private founders may operate quietly for years with limited public attention. Once a company enters public markets, however, visibility increases dramatically. Financial media begins analyzing company performance continuously. Institutional investors evaluate every quarterly report. Analysts publish projections and recommendations. Journalists monitor executive behavior. Social media commentary intensifies.

Public founders often become public figures almost overnight.

This increased visibility creates emotional pressure because company performance becomes tied directly to public perception. A single earnings report may influence billions of dollars in market value within hours. Stock price fluctuations may dominate headlines regardless of whether the company's long-term fundamentals remain strong.

This environment can become emotionally exhausting.

Many founders who thrived privately struggle initially with the emotional volatility of public markets because stock prices fluctuate constantly for reasons beyond operational control. Macroeconomic conditions, interest rates, investor sentiment, geopolitical events, analyst expectations, industry trends, and algorithmic trading may all affect stock performance independently of actual company execution.

Sophisticated founders eventually learn an important lesson:

Stock price and enterprise value are not always identical in the short term.

Public markets can become emotional, irrational, euphoric, or fearful temporarily. Founders who obsess over daily market fluctuations often experience severe psychological stress. Strong public company leaders therefore learn how to focus on long-term operational execution while maintaining emotional stability during periods of volatility.

Another major transformation involves time horizon compression. Private founders often think in multi-year development cycles. Public markets, however, introduce quarterly reporting structures that encourage shorter-term measurement. Analysts evaluate earnings growth, margins, customer acquisition, guidance projections, and operational metrics every quarter.

This creates tension between long-term innovation and short-term expectations.

Founders may feel pressure to prioritize quarterly performance even when long-term strategic investments require patience. Research and development, international expansion, infrastructure scaling, acquisitions, and innovation initiatives may temporarily reduce profitability despite strengthening long-term value creation.

Public founders must therefore balance two competing responsibilities simultaneously:

Delivering consistent quarterly execution while protecting long-term strategic vision.

This balancing act defines elite public company leadership.

Another major psychological challenge involves loss of control.

Private founders often maintain substantial authority over company decisions. Public companies, however, introduce broader governance obligations involving institutional shareholders, independent boards, regulatory oversight, and fiduciary responsibilities.

Founders accustomed to unilateral decision-making may struggle emotionally with increased accountability structures.

Sophisticated founders recognize that governance evolution is necessary as companies scale. Public market investors require transparency, compliance, financial discipline, and operational consistency because large amounts of institutional capital become involved.

This is why founder maturity matters enormously during IPO transitions.

The leadership behaviors effective during startup stages may not remain effective during public company operations. Public CEOs must communicate clearly with investors, regulators, employees, analysts, and boards simultaneously while maintaining operational focus.

Communication becomes one of the most critical public company skills.

Every statement matters. Public executives must think carefully about earnings calls, interviews, press releases, investor conferences, forecasts, and guidance statements because markets react rapidly to perceived signals.

This creates psychological intensity few private founders fully anticipate.

One sentence during an earnings call can erase billions in market capitalization.

At the same time, public markets also create enormous opportunities.

Access to public capital can accelerate expansion dramatically. Publicly traded stock can be used for acquisitions, executive recruitment, employee compensation, strategic partnerships, and financial flexibility.

IPO visibility can also strengthen brand credibility significantly.

Customers, institutional partners, media organizations, and global investors often view public companies as more stable and established. This increased legitimacy may improve customer trust, recruiting capability, and strategic positioning.

However, public market visibility also magnifies weaknesses.

Operational mistakes become public quickly. Missed earnings targets attract criticism. Internal cultural problems may become visible externally. Regulatory scrutiny increases significantly.

This is why operational readiness is essential before pursuing public offerings.

Many founders become overly focused on achieving IPO status itself rather than preparing for the realities of operating publicly afterward.

An IPO is not the finish line.

It is the beginning of an entirely different phase of leadership.

Another major transformation involves wealth psychology.

When companies go public successfully, founders often experience dramatic increases in net worth. Stock ownership may suddenly create immense paper wealth. Media outlets may describe founders as billionaires overnight.

Yet this experience can become psychologically complicated.

Public market wealth fluctuates constantly. Daily stock movements may increase or decrease founder net worth by enormous amounts. Founders who attach emotional stability directly to stock price movements often experience anxiety, obsession, or emotional exhaustion. Sophisticated founders eventually learn emotional detachment from short-term valuation swings.

They understand that public markets move in cycles.

Bull markets create euphoria.

Bear markets create fear.

Neither necessarily reflects long-term company potential accurately.

Another important psychological challenge is identity evolution.

Many founders build their identities around startup survival. The early entrepreneurial journey involves intensity, scarcity, creativity, speed, and constant problem-solving. Once companies become public, the environment changes dramatically.

Processes become more structured.

Organizations become larger.

Governance becomes formalized.

Decision-making often slows.

Some founders struggle emotionally because the company no longer feels like the small mission-driven startup they originally created. This transition can create feelings of disconnection.

Sophisticated founders prepare emotionally for organizational evolution long before public offerings occur. They understand that scaling companies requires changing systems, structures, and leadership approaches over time.

Another major concept public founders must understand is institutional ownership behavior.

Public companies attract various shareholder types including hedge funds, pension funds, mutual funds, sovereign wealth funds, retail investors, activist investors, and index funds. Each group may have different incentives, time horizons, and expectations.

Some investors prioritize long-term growth.

Others prioritize short-term profitability.

Some seek operational efficiency.

Others seek aggressive expansion.

Public company leadership therefore requires navigating diverse investor expectations simultaneously.

This complexity can become politically and emotionally demanding.

Activist investors create another layer of public market psychology.

Activist investors may pressure companies to change leadership, restructure operations, pursue acquisitions, sell divisions, repurchase shares, reduce costs, or alter strategy. Some activism improves shareholder value constructively. Other forms create conflict and instability.

Founders operating public companies must therefore develop resilience and strategic communication discipline.

Another important public market concept involves guidance management.

Public companies often provide forward-looking projections regarding revenue growth, margins, profitability, or operational performance. Markets react strongly when companies exceed or miss these expectations.

As a result, founders must balance optimism with realism carefully.

Overpromising can damage credibility severely.

Underpromising may weaken investor enthusiasm.

Managing expectations becomes a strategic discipline.

Another major transition involves employee psychology after IPOs.

Public offerings often create life-changing financial outcomes for employees holding stock options or equity compensation. While this can improve morale temporarily, it may also create unexpected cultural shifts.

Some employees lose motivation after achieving financial security.

Others become distracted by stock price monitoring.

Some leave the company entirely after lock-up periods expire.

Sophisticated founders therefore focus heavily on maintaining mission alignment after IPOs occur.

Mission becomes especially important because financial incentives alone rarely sustain long-term organizational culture.

Another challenge public founders face involves media narratives.

Public companies constantly face external interpretation from analysts, journalists, influencers, and financial commentators.

Narratives may shift rapidly based on market conditions, industry trends, or temporary operational changes. Founders who become emotionally reactive to media cycles often struggle psychologically.

Strong public leaders maintain long-term focus despite external noise.

Another critical area involves legal and regulatory pressure.

Public companies operate under significantly greater compliance obligations involving securities law, financial disclosures, insider trading restrictions, governance requirements, and shareholder protections.

Regulatory mistakes can create severe consequences.

Founders must therefore build sophisticated legal, accounting, investor relations, and compliance infrastructure.

Another major transformation involves succession thinking.

Private founders often operate indefinitely without formal succession planning. Public markets, however, increasingly evaluate leadership continuity, executive depth, and organizational resilience beyond the founder personally.

This forces founders to think beyond themselves operationally.

Companies dependent entirely on one individual may face lower investor confidence. Sophisticated founders therefore build strong executive teams capable of sustaining long-term operational performance.

This leadership maturity strengthens enterprise value significantly.

One of the most overlooked truths about IPOs is that public markets do not solve operational weakness.

Public markets amplify both strengths and weaknesses.

Strong businesses may scale dramatically with public capital access.

Weak businesses may collapse under public scrutiny.

This is why foundational operational quality matters so much before public offerings occur.

Another critical lesson is that public company leadership requires emotional endurance.

Stock volatility, media pressure, activist scrutiny, investor expectations, employee dynamics, regulatory oversight, and competitive intensity create constant psychological demands.

Founders who survive successfully in public markets often develop extraordinary emotional discipline. They learn patience.

They learn communication control.

They learn strategic focus.

They learn emotional resilience during both market euphoria and market panic.

Ultimately, going public represents far more than a financial transaction.

It represents a complete transformation in leadership psychology, operational structure, communication responsibility, and wealth management.

The founders who thrive after IPOs are usually not those most obsessed with stock prices.

They are the founders who understand how to balance long-term vision with public market accountability.

They understand that sustainable enterprise value is built through operational excellence, disciplined execution, strategic communication, and emotional resilience.

Most importantly, they recognize that becoming a public company is not the final achievement.

It is simply the next stage in building enduring influence, scalable enterprise value, and long-term wealth through capital markets.

And mastering that transition is what separates temporary market success from lasting public company leadership.

The Morning the Bell Rang

At 5:12 a.m., Noah Bennett stood alone inside his New York hotel suite staring out over the city skyline while the rest of Manhattan remained mostly asleep.

In just a few hours, his company would officially begin trading on the public markets.

The thought felt surreal.

For nearly thirteen years, Noah had lived inside the chaos of entrepreneurship. He had survived cash shortages, failed product launches, investor rejections, legal battles, hiring disasters, market crashes, and brutal competitive pressure while building his cloud infrastructure company from a tiny startup into one of the fastest-growing technology businesses in the world.

Now the IPO had finally arrived.

Financial news networks were already discussing the company nonstop. Analysts predicted one of the largest technology public offerings of the year. Investors from around the world prepared to buy shares the moment trading opened.

From the outside, it looked like the happiest day of Noah's life.

Privately, however, he felt overwhelmed.

He barely slept the night before.

His mind raced constantly between excitement and anxiety. One moment he imagined the opportunities ahead—global expansion, acquisitions, financial freedom, long-term impact. The next moment he feared disappointing public investors, losing company culture, or becoming trapped inside endless market expectations.

The transition already felt different.

Just months earlier, Noah operated relatively privately. Now every comment, interview, and financial projection carried enormous consequences. Journalists followed him constantly. Analysts dissected company metrics publicly. Investors speculated about future growth rates before each earnings report even existed.

For the first time in his career, Noah realized the company no longer belonged only to him and his team.

It now belonged partly to the market. At 7:30 a.m., Noah arrived at the stock exchange surrounded by executives, bankers, lawyers, and employees. Cameras flashed constantly as reporters shouted questions from behind barricades.

Employees smiled excitedly.

Investors celebrated.

Media outlets called the IPO historic.

But Noah noticed something strange.

The closer they moved toward the opening bell ceremony, the quieter he became emotionally.

During the final preparation meeting before trading began, his CFO leaned over and whispered, "You okay?"

Noah forced a smile.

"I think so."

But internally, he wasn't sure.

The IPO represented more than financial success. It represented the end of one identity and the beginning of another. The startup founder who once worked from tiny apartments and lived entirely in survival mode was disappearing.

Now he would become a public company CEO.

That realization felt heavier than he expected.

Minutes later, the exchange floor erupted with energy as the countdown began.

Ten.

Nine.

Eight.

Employees cheered loudly.

Seven.

Six.

Cameras pointed directly at Noah.

Five.

Four.

His hands felt cold.

Three.

Two.

One. The bell rang. Applause exploded across the trading floor while giant digital screens displayed the company ticker symbol publicly for the first time.

The stock surged immediately.

Financial media celebrated the opening price as a massive success. Reporters rushed toward executives asking for reactions. Employees cried emotionally while hugging one another.

Noah smiled for the cameras.

But internally, something strange happened.

Instead of feeling finished, he suddenly felt exposed.

For years, the company's struggles remained mostly private. Now every future challenge would unfold publicly in front of investors, analysts, employees, and media organizations worldwide.

That reality hit him harder than expected.

The following months became emotionally exhausting.

The company remained operationally strong, but public market volatility created constant psychological noise. Some days the stock climbed dramatically based on analyst optimism. Other days it dropped sharply due to macroeconomic concerns unrelated to company performance.

Noah became obsessed with checking stock prices constantly.

Every morning started with market updates.

Every earnings report created anxiety.

Every analyst note affected his mood.

Eventually, his wife confronted him gently one evening after dinner.

"You're letting the market decide whether you feel successful," she told him quietly.

The sentence unsettled him deeply because he knew it was true.

Noah had unconsciously attached emotional stability to daily stock movements. When the market praised the company, he felt powerful. When the stock declined, he questioned himself constantly—even when operational execution remained strong.

He realized public markets were controlling his psychology.

That realization changed everything.

Over time, Noah deliberately retrained his thinking. Instead of focusing on short-term stock fluctuations, he redirected attention toward long-term fundamentals: customer retention, infrastructure quality, innovation, operational scalability, and leadership development.

He stopped checking stock prices obsessively.

He reduced media consumption.

He focused on building.

Ironically, once he became less emotionally reactive to public market noise, his leadership improved dramatically.

Employees noticed the difference.

Board meetings became calmer.

Strategic decisions became more disciplined.

Long-term thinking returned.

Years later, the company became one of the dominant infrastructure businesses in global cloud computing. The stock experienced massive volatility during that period—booms, crashes, recoveries, analyst upgrades, downgrades, economic crises, and technological shifts.

But Noah's psychology evolved permanently.

He finally understood something that most public founders learn only after emotional struggle: The market has a price for your company every day.

That does not mean the market fully understands its value every day.

At a leadership conference years later, a young founder preparing for an IPO nervously asked Noah what the hardest part of going public really was.

Noah thought quietly for a moment before answering.

"Learning how to lead while millions of people judge your company in real time."

The audience laughed softly.

But Noah continued.

"Private founders build companies. Public founders learn how to protect vision while surviving pressure."

Then he smiled slightly before sharing the lesson that transformed his own leadership after the IPO.

"If your emotions rise and fall with the stock price, the market owns more than your shares. It owns your peace of mind."

Chapter 7

Founder Stock Sales, Secondary Markets, and Strategic Liquidity Before the Exit

One of the most misunderstood areas of founder wealth creation involves secondary liquidity. Many entrepreneurs believe wealth only becomes real after a full acquisition or IPO. In reality, some of the most sophisticated founders strategically create liquidity long before traditional exits occur. They understand that managing personal financial risk is just as important as growing enterprise value.

Secondary liquidity refers to the sale of existing shares by founders, employees, or early investors before a company experiences a full public offering or acquisition. Unlike primary fundraising, where companies issue new shares to raise fresh capital, secondary transactions involve the transfer of already existing ownership between shareholders and buyers.

This distinction is extremely important.

Primary financing brings money into the company itself.

Secondary financing brings money directly to shareholders. For founders, secondary liquidity can become one of the most powerful financial and psychological tools in entrepreneurship when approached strategically.

Many founders spend years building companies while remaining almost entirely illiquid. Their net worth may appear massive on paper, yet they often live under constant financial pressure because their wealth remains inaccessible. The company may be worth hundreds of millions of dollars, but if ownership cannot easily be converted into cash, the founder may still experience stress surrounding mortgages, family obligations, taxes, lifestyle expenses, or long-term security.

This creates an unusual paradox.

A founder may technically be wealthy while simultaneously feeling financially vulnerable.

Sophisticated entrepreneurs eventually realize that personal financial stability can improve leadership quality dramatically. Founders constantly operating under financial stress may make emotional decisions, accept poor investment terms, reject healthy acquisitions out of desperation for larger outcomes, or become psychologically overwhelmed by uncertainty.

Strategic liquidity helps solve this problem.

By selling a relatively small portion of ownership during growth stages, founders can reduce personal financial pressure while maintaining substantial upside participation in the company's future success.

This balance becomes critical.

Many inexperienced entrepreneurs assume that selling any shares before a full exit signals weakness or lack of confidence. In reality, sophisticated investors often encourage reasonable founder liquidity because emotionally stable founders usually make better long-term decisions.

The key word is reasonable.

Excessive early selling can absolutely create concern. If founders aggressively liquidate large portions of ownership too early, investors may question long-term commitment or confidence in future growth. However, modest secondary liquidity designed to reduce personal risk and create stability is often viewed positively by experienced institutional investors.

Understanding timing is essential.

Secondary markets usually become available only after companies achieve meaningful traction, investor demand, or later-stage financing maturity. Early-stage startups generally lack sufficient liquidity infrastructure because valuations remain uncertain and risk remains extremely high. As companies grow, however, secondary opportunities often emerge through venture capital transactions, growth equity rounds, private secondary marketplaces, institutional investors, or recapitalization structures.

This is where founder wealth strategy becomes increasingly sophisticated.

Some founders intentionally structure fundraising rounds that include both primary and secondary components. Investors may provide fresh growth capital to the company while simultaneously purchasing limited shares directly from founders or early employees.

This creates multiple benefits simultaneously.

The company receives capital for expansion.

Founders receive partial liquidity.

Employees may gain financial rewards.

Investor relationships strengthen.

Psychological pressure decreases.

Operational focus improves.

Sophisticated founders understand that entrepreneurship is not only a financial game but also an emotional endurance challenge. Personal liquidity can dramatically improve emotional resilience because founders no longer feel trapped entirely inside uncertain future outcomes.

One major psychological transformation occurs when founders stop operating from survival fear.

Entrepreneurs with no liquidity often feel emotionally cornered. Every market fluctuation, fundraising challenge, or operational setback may feel catastrophic because personal financial security depends entirely on future success.

Partial liquidity changes this dynamic.

A founder who secures even moderate financial stability may become calmer, more strategic, more patient, and less emotionally reactive. Ironically, reducing desperation often improves long-term company performance significantly.

This is why many elite investors quietly prefer founders with some financial breathing room.

Another important concept involves diversification.

Many founders become excessively concentrated in a single asset: their company stock. While concentration often creates wealth initially, long-term wealth preservation usually requires diversification eventually. No matter how promising a company appears, risk always exists.

Industries change.

Technology evolves.

Competition intensifies.

Regulations shift.

Economic cycles fluctuate.

Even exceptional businesses may experience volatility or unexpected disruption.

Sophisticated founders therefore understand the importance of gradually converting concentrated equity positions into diversified assets over time.

This does not mean abandoning belief in the company.

It means understanding risk management intelligently.

For example, a founder worth fifty million dollars entirely through private company equity may actually possess fragile wealth because one negative market event could dramatically reduce valuation. A founder who strategically diversifies portions of liquidity into real estate, public markets, fixed income assets, private investments, or cash reserves often achieves greater long-term stability.

Wealth creation and wealth preservation are different disciplines.

Secondary liquidity helps bridge these disciplines.

Another major area founders must understand involves employee secondary sales.

As startups mature, employees holding stock options or equity compensation may also seek liquidity opportunities. Many early employees dedicate years to high-growth companies while accepting lower salaries in exchange for future equity upside.

Secondary markets can reward these employees before traditional exits occur.

This creates morale benefits, retention advantages, and stronger organizational loyalty when managed correctly.

However, companies must structure employee liquidity carefully because uncontrolled secondary activity can create cultural instability or cap table complexity.

Sophisticated founders therefore develop clear liquidity policies balancing employee incentives with long-term organizational health. Another important concept is valuation discipline.

Secondary transactions often occur at negotiated private market valuations. During periods of market optimism, private company valuations may rise dramatically due to investor enthusiasm. However, inflated valuations can create unrealistic expectations and future challenges.

Founders must therefore evaluate secondary opportunities carefully rather than emotionally chasing maximum paper valuations.

A slightly lower but realistic valuation may create healthier long-term outcomes than inflated pricing disconnected from operational fundamentals.

This is especially important because secondary transactions often influence future fundraising expectations and investor perception.

Another key area involves information asymmetry.

Private markets operate differently from public markets because information remains less transparent. Buyers evaluating secondary shares often rely heavily on founder communication, operational reporting, investor confidence, and growth projections.

This creates ethical responsibilities.

Sophisticated founders maintain transparency and integrity during secondary transactions because reputation compounds over time. Misleading investors, exaggerating projections, or creating artificial hype may generate short-term gains but damage long-term credibility severely.

Trust becomes extremely valuable in private capital markets.

Another major form of strategic liquidity involves recapitalization transactions.

In recapitalizations, private equity firms or institutional investors purchase substantial ownership stakes while founders retain meaningful operational control and future upside participation.

These transactions often occur in mature private businesses generating strong cash flow.

For example, a founder may sell forty percent ownership to private equity, receive substantial personal liquidity, and continue leading the business operationally. Future growth may then generate additional wealth through the remaining ownership position.

This hybrid approach has become increasingly common because it balances liquidity with continued upside participation.

Some founders use recapitalizations to “de-risk” financially while maintaining entrepreneurial momentum.

Another important concept is tax planning surrounding secondary sales.

Taxes can dramatically affect realized liquidity outcomes. Capital gains structures, state tax exposure, trust planning, timing strategies, qualified small business stock treatment, charitable planning, and residency considerations all influence final results significantly.

Sophisticated founders plan liquidity long before transactions occur.

They build relationships with tax advisors, estate planners, and legal professionals capable of structuring wealth intelligently.

Poor planning can destroy enormous amounts of wealth unnecessarily.

Another major psychological challenge founders face during secondary liquidity is guilt.

Some entrepreneurs feel emotionally conflicted about taking personal liquidity while employees continue working intensely toward future exits. Others fear investor judgment or media perception. These emotions are common but often misguided.

Founders who completely neglect personal financial security may unintentionally weaken long-term leadership quality. Burnout, stress, family pressure, and emotional exhaustion can damage both founders and companies over time.

Reasonable liquidity creates sustainability.

Another important lesson involves lifestyle inflation.

Some founders experience sudden liquidity and dramatically increase spending immediately. Luxury purchases, oversized homes, speculative investments, social pressure, and status-driven consumption may create instability quickly.

Sophisticated founders approach liquidity with discipline.

They understand that preserving wealth matters just as much as creating it.

Many of the world's most financially successful founders maintain surprisingly conservative lifestyles during growth phases because they prioritize optionality, flexibility, and long-term strategic freedom over short-term consumption.

Another critical aspect of secondary liquidity is negotiation leverage.

Founders with strong operational businesses and healthy cash positions often negotiate secondary terms from positions of strength. Founders under financial stress may accept unfavorable pricing, restrictive structures, or weak governance protections simply to obtain liquidity.

This again highlights why operational discipline matters so much.

Strong businesses create founder leverage.

Leverage improves liquidity outcomes.

Another evolving area involves secondary marketplaces.

Over the last decade, private secondary markets have expanded significantly. Specialized firms, institutional platforms, venture funds, and private exchanges increasingly facilitate private share transactions in late-stage companies.

This evolution is changing entrepreneurship itself.

Historically, founders often waited a decade or longer for liquidity through IPOs or acquisitions. Today, strategic secondary liquidity may occur much earlier for successful companies.

This changes how founders approach risk, scaling, and long-term planning.

However, founders must still balance liquidity carefully with commitment.

Entrepreneurial success requires long-term alignment. Founders who become overly focused on personal monetization too early may damage culture, investor confidence, and strategic discipline.

The strongest founders balance personal security with continued long-term ownership conviction.

Ultimately, secondary liquidity represents far more than simply "selling shares."

It represents strategic risk management.

It represents emotional sustainability.

It represents wealth preservation.

It represents psychological stability.

And when handled intelligently, it allows founders to continue building aggressively from positions of strength rather than fear.

The entrepreneurs who create lasting wealth are often not those who remain blindly concentrated forever. They are the founders who understand when to hold, when to diversify, when to create liquidity, and how to preserve optionality while continuing to participate in future upside.

Because founder wealth is not simply about reaching one giant exit someday.

It is about building long-term financial freedom intelligently throughout the entire entrepreneurial journey.

And mastering strategic liquidity is one of the most important skills within that process.

The Founder Who Finally Slept Peacefully

For nearly eight years, Adrian Morales carried stress so constantly that he no longer recognized what calm felt like.

From the outside, his life looked extraordinary.

He had built one of the fastest-growing logistics software companies in the country. Venture capital firms praised the company publicly. Industry conferences invited him to speak constantly. Financial articles described his startup as a future billion-dollar platform disrupting global transportation infrastructure.

Employees admired him.

Investors respected him. Competitors feared him. Yet privately, Adrian felt trapped.

Every dollar of his net worth existed almost entirely inside private company stock. Technically, his ownership stake made him extremely wealthy on paper. But paper wealth did not help him sleep at night.

His parents still lived in a modest apartment.

He delayed getting married because of financial uncertainty.

He worried constantly about market conditions, fundraising environments, and operational setbacks because one major failure could erase nearly everything.

Friends assumed Adrian was rich.

In reality, he felt financially fragile.

The pressure intensified after the company's rapid expansion during its sixth year. Revenue exploded, but so did operational complexity. Payroll grew enormous. Investor expectations increased aggressively. Media attention became relentless.

Every quarter carried emotional weight. Adrian became obsessed with the company's future valuation because his entire identity and financial security depended on one outcome: a massive exit someday.

Then the market shifted unexpectedly.

Technology valuations dropped sharply across the industry. Several high-profile startups collapsed. Venture funding slowed dramatically. Suddenly, companies that once raised capital easily struggled to secure financing.

For the first time in years, Adrian experienced genuine fear.

Not because the company itself was weak—the business remained operationally strong—but because he realized how dangerously concentrated his life had become.

One company.

One asset.

One future outcome.

Everything depended on it.

The realization haunted him.

During a private dinner with another founder named Elaine, Adrian finally admitted how exhausted he felt emotionally. Elaine listened carefully before asking a question that completely changed his perspective.

"How much of your stress comes from the business," she asked quietly, "and how much comes from having zero personal liquidity?"

The question stunned him because he immediately knew the answer.

Most of the pressure came from feeling financially trapped.

Elaine explained that years earlier she sold a small percentage of her shares during a late-stage secondary transaction. She still retained substantial ownership and upside participation, but the partial liquidity transformed her psychology completely.

"You lead differently when survival pressure disappears," she told him.

Adrian resisted the idea initially.

Selling shares felt emotionally wrong. Part of him believed true founders should never sell before a final exit. Another part feared investors would question his confidence.

Still, the conversation stayed in his mind constantly afterward.

Weeks later, one of the company's growth-stage investors approached Adrian privately about a secondary opportunity. The investor proposed purchasing a relatively small portion of Adrian's shares during an upcoming financing round.

The numbers were life-changing.

Yet Adrian still hesitated emotionally.

For days he stared at spreadsheets trying to calculate future upside scenarios. What if the company became ten times larger later? What if he regretted selling even a small percentage? What if employees viewed the decision negatively?

Finally, after multiple conversations with advisors, Adrian realized something important.

He was treating liquidity emotionally instead of strategically.

Selling a small percentage would not destroy his future upside. It would create stability.

The transaction closed quietly two months later.

Almost immediately, Adrian's life changed in ways he never expected.

He paid off his parents' mortgage completely.

He diversified modestly into real estate and conservative investments.

He created financial security for his future family.

Most importantly, for the first time in nearly a decade, he stopped operating from fear.

The psychological shift was enormous.

Before the liquidity event, every business setback felt catastrophic because his entire future depended on one outcome. Afterward, he still cared deeply about the company—but desperation disappeared.

Ironically, the company performed better afterward.

Adrian became calmer during board meetings.

He made more rational strategic decisions.

He stopped obsessing over short-term valuation fluctuations.

He focused more clearly on long-term operational quality instead of constantly chasing external validation.

Employees noticed the difference immediately.

The culture improved.

Leadership communication became more stable.

Execution quality strengthened.

Years later, the company eventually completed a successful IPO at a valuation far beyond what Adrian once imagined possible. Because he retained substantial ownership, the IPO still generated enormous wealth.

But privately, Adrian understood something most outsiders never would.

The most important financial decision of his entrepreneurial life was not the IPO itself.

It was the moment he stopped allowing fear to control his leadership.

At a founder retreat years later, a younger entrepreneur nervously asked Adrian whether founders should ever sell shares before a final exit.

Adrian smiled quietly before answering.

"Most founders think liquidity is about money," he said. "It's actually about psychology."

The room became silent.

Then Adrian explained the lesson he learned through years of pressure and concentration risk.

"When your entire life depends on one future event, fear eventually controls your decisions. Strategic liquidity gives you something more valuable than money."

The young founder leaned forward carefully.

"What's that?" he asked.

Adrian smiled slightly.

"The ability to think clearly again."

[illegible]

Creating wealth and preserving wealth are two entirely different disciplines. Many founders spend years learning how to build companies, scale operations, attract investors, increase valuation, and engineer liquidity events. Yet surprisingly few entrepreneurs dedicate equal attention to what happens after wealth is created. This oversight can become extremely costly because taxes, legal exposure, poor planning, emotional spending, and inadequate wealth structures can rapidly erode fortunes that took decades to build.

The transition from wealth creation to wealth preservation represents one of the most important psychological and financial shifts in a founder's life.

Entrepreneurs are often trained to think aggressively. During company-building stages, risk-taking, rapid concentration, and relentless reinvestment are rewarded. But after a major liquidity event, preserving wealth requires a different mindset entirely. Wealth preservation emphasizes structure,

Chapter 8

Taxes, Trusts, Estate Planning, and Protecting Founder Wealth Across Generations

Creating wealth and preserving wealth are two entirely different disciplines. Many founders spend years learning how to build companies, scale operations, attract investors, increase valuation, and engineer liquidity events. Yet surprisingly few entrepreneurs dedicate equal attention to what happens after wealth is created. This oversight can become extremely costly because taxes, legal exposure, poor planning, emotional spending, and inadequate wealth structures can rapidly erode fortunes that took decades to build.

The transition from wealth creation to wealth preservation represents one of the most important psychological and financial shifts in a founder's life.

Entrepreneurs are often trained to think aggressively. During company-building stages, risk-taking, speed, concentration, and relentless reinvestment are rewarded. But after major liquidity events occur, preserving wealth requires a different mindset entirely. Wealth preservation emphasizes structure, patience, diversification, tax efficiency, legal protection, long-term planning, and intergenerational strategy.

Founders who fail to make this transition often lose wealth surprisingly quickly.

History is filled with entrepreneurs, athletes, entertainers, executives, and investors who created enormous fortunes but failed to preserve them across decades or generations. Excessive concentration, poor tax planning, reckless spending, lawsuits, family conflict, weak estate structures, and emotional decision-making can destroy wealth rapidly if proper systems are not established.

Sophisticated founders therefore begin thinking about wealth preservation long before major exits occur.

One of the most important areas of wealth preservation is taxation.

Taxes may become one of the single largest expenses founders ever face after liquidity events. Acquisitions, IPOs, secondary sales, stock compensation exercises, and recapitalizations can create enormous taxable gains. Without careful planning, founders may lose substantial percentages of wealth unnecessarily.

This is why proactive tax strategy matters so much. Sophisticated founders do not wait until after liquidity events occur to think about taxes. They structure ownership, residency, trusts, charitable entities, and investment strategies years beforehand whenever possible.

Capital gains taxes are one of the first major concepts founders must understand.

When founders sell appreciated stock or ownership interests, the profits generated may be taxed as capital gains rather than ordinary income depending on structure and holding periods. Long-term capital gains rates are often lower than ordinary income tax rates, which can significantly affect realized wealth.

However, taxation becomes far more complex once wealth reaches substantial scale.

State taxes, international exposure, alternative minimum tax considerations, stock option treatment, trust structures, charitable deductions, carried interest rules, estate taxes, and residency planning all influence outcomes dramatically.

A founder who ignores these complexities may unknowingly create avoidable financial losses.

Another major wealth preservation tool involves Qualified Small Business Stock, often referred to as QSBS in the United

States. Under certain conditions, founders and early investors may qualify for significant capital gains exclusions on qualified startup stock holdings if shares are held for specific time periods and meet legal requirements.

This can create enormous tax advantages.

Some founders save millions or even tens of millions of dollars through proper QSBS planning.

However, qualification rules are highly technical, which is why sophisticated legal and tax guidance becomes essential.

Another foundational area of wealth preservation involves trusts.

Trusts are legal structures designed to hold, manage, transfer, or protect assets under specified conditions. Many founders initially assume trusts are only for ultra-wealthy families, but in reality, trusts can become critically important tools for tax planning, asset protection, estate management, and generational wealth preservation.

Trusts allow founders to structure wealth intentionally.

Some trusts help reduce estate taxes.

Others protect assets from lawsuits or creditors.

Some support charitable goals. Others preserve wealth for future generations.

Sophisticated founders often establish trusts long before liquidity events because transferring assets before valuation increases may create significant long-term tax advantages.

Irrevocable trusts are especially important in advanced wealth planning.

Unlike revocable trusts, irrevocable structures generally remove assets from the founder's taxable estate once properly transferred. This may reduce future estate tax exposure dramatically if assets appreciate significantly over time.

For example, a founder transferring shares into an irrevocable trust before a major liquidity event may shift future appreciation outside the taxable estate structure. Over decades, this planning can preserve enormous amounts of wealth for future generations.

Another important strategy involves Grantor Retained Annuity Trusts, or GRATs.

GRATs allow founders to transfer appreciating assets to heirs while potentially minimizing gift and estate tax consequences. These structures became popular among technology founders and high-growth entrepreneurs because rapidly appreciating equity can create substantial wealth transfer opportunities when structured correctly. Family Limited Partnerships and Family Offices also play major roles in founder wealth preservation.

Family offices are private organizations established to manage large-scale family wealth. These structures may oversee investments, tax planning, estate administration, philanthropy, legal coordination, risk management, and multigenerational governance.

Some founders initially believe family offices are only necessary for billionaires, but even moderate large-scale liquidity events may justify institutional wealth management structures.

The larger the wealth becomes, the more sophisticated coordination usually becomes necessary.

Another major consideration is asset protection.

Founders who achieve significant liquidity often become targets for lawsuits, business disputes, opportunistic claims, or financial predation. Asset protection planning helps shield wealth through legal structures, insurance strategies, entity separation, and trust planning.

This is not about hiding assets illegally.

It is about structuring wealth responsibly and defensively within legal frameworks.

Sophisticated founders understand that protecting wealth requires intentional legal architecture.

Another essential wealth preservation area involves diversification.

During wealth creation phases, concentration often creates extraordinary returns. Founders may hold most net worth in a single company. However, after liquidity events, maintaining extreme concentration may create unnecessary risk.

Markets fluctuate.

Industries change.

Technological disruption occurs constantly.

Sophisticated founders therefore transition gradually from concentrated entrepreneurial risk toward diversified capital preservation strategies.

Diversification may include public equities, real estate, private investments, fixed income assets, venture capital exposure, international holdings, infrastructure investments, and alternative assets.

The goal shifts from maximizing growth at all costs toward balancing growth with stability and long-term preservation.

Another critical issue is emotional spending.

Sudden wealth can create psychological disorientation. Founders who spent years operating under scarcity may overcompensate after liquidity events through excessive consumption, luxury purchases, speculative investments, social pressure, or lifestyle inflation.

Without discipline, even substantial fortunes may deteriorate rapidly.

Sophisticated founders understand that wealth preservation requires emotional maturity.

Some of the world's wealthiest entrepreneurs continue living relatively disciplined lifestyles despite enormous financial capacity because they prioritize flexibility, optionality, and long-term stability over short-term status displays.

Another important concept is intergenerational wealth education.

Many fortunes disappear not because the original founder lacked intelligence, but because future generations lacked preparation. Children inheriting wealth without financial education, emotional maturity, or responsibility may struggle significantly. This is why sophisticated founders often focus heavily on values, education, governance, and family culture in addition to financial structures.

True generational wealth is not only financial.

It is intellectual, emotional, cultural, and strategic.

Some founders intentionally involve family members gradually in business operations, philanthropy, investing, governance discussions, or entrepreneurial education to strengthen long-term stewardship.

Another increasingly important area is philanthropy.

Many founders eventually recognize that wealth creates not only opportunity but also responsibility. Philanthropy allows entrepreneurs to support causes aligned with personal values while also creating potential tax planning benefits.

Charitable foundations, donor-advised funds, charitable remainder trusts, and nonprofit organizations all represent vehicles through which founders may create social impact while structuring wealth intelligently.

Some entrepreneurs discover that philanthropy provides meaning beyond financial accumulation itself.

Another critical wealth preservation concept involves residency and jurisdiction planning. Taxes vary dramatically between states and countries. Sophisticated founders sometimes relocate strategically before major liquidity events or structure international holdings carefully to improve tax efficiency legally.

However, these strategies require careful planning because residency rules, domicile tests, and international tax obligations can become extremely complex.

Improper planning may create severe legal and financial consequences.

This again reinforces the importance of experienced advisors.

Another important issue involves succession planning.

Many founders delay succession discussions because they identify deeply with leadership roles. However, preserving wealth across generations often requires preparing organizations, investments, family structures, and governance systems beyond the founder personally.

Without succession planning, wealth fragmentation and operational instability may occur after leadership transitions.

Sophisticated founders think long term. They recognize that

wealth preservation is not merely about personal comfort but about creating durable systems capable of surviving beyond individual lifetimes. Another major consideration involves privacy and security.

As founder wealth grows, visibility often increases. Media attention, public filings, social exposure, and digital vulnerability may create security concerns. Sophisticated wealth preservation therefore includes cybersecurity, privacy protection, legal confidentiality structures, and physical security planning when necessary.

Modern wealth management increasingly involves digital risk management as well.

Another important lesson founders eventually learn is that money amplifies existing psychology.

Wealth itself does not automatically create happiness, wisdom, discipline, or fulfillment. Founders carrying unresolved emotional patterns before liquidity events often continue carrying those patterns afterward—sometimes magnified by larger financial consequences.

This is why emotional intelligence matters deeply in wealth preservation.

Founders who develop healthy relationships with money, identity, purpose, and responsibility often preserve wealth more successfully over time than those driven primarily by ego, insecurity, or external validation.

Another key concept is long-term investment philosophy.

Some founders lose wealth after liquidity events because they continue behaving like concentrated startup operators within diversified wealth environments. Excessive speculation, overconfidence, or reckless leverage can destroy fortunes surprisingly quickly.

Sophisticated wealth preservation requires patience and discipline.

Compounding becomes extremely powerful once large capital bases exist.

Protecting downside risk becomes just as important as pursuing upside opportunity.

Ultimately, protecting founder wealth across generations requires intentional structure.

It requires understanding taxes, trusts, diversification, legal protection, governance, succession planning, philanthropy, emotional discipline, and long-term thinking.

The founders who preserve wealth most effectively are often not the flashiest or most aggressive after liquidity events.

They are the founders who recognize that true wealth is not simply about how much money is created.

It is about how intelligently that wealth is structured, protected, transferred, and used over decades and generations.

Because creating wealth may change one life.

But preserving wealth intelligently has the potential to change many lives far into the future.

And that is where founder wealth creation ultimately becomes legacy building.

The Billionaire Who Feared Losing Everything

When Victor Hale sold his cybersecurity company for nearly four billion dollars, the world assumed his problems had ended forever.

Financial news networks called him one of the youngest self-made billionaires in the country. Magazine covers praised his brilliance. Investors invited him into elite financial circles almost immediately. Luxury real estate brokers flooded his phone with offers for waterfront estates, penthouses, and private retreats.

From the outside, Victor appeared unstoppable.

But privately, something unexpected happened after the acquisition closed. He became terrified. For nearly fifteen years, Victor understood exactly how to create value. He knew how to build teams, raise capital, scale technology, negotiate contracts, survive competition, and grow enterprise valuation aggressively.

But now, for the first time in his life, he faced a completely different challenge:

How do you protect wealth large enough to disappear through one generation of bad decisions?

The thought consumed him constantly.

Before the acquisition, life felt simpler psychologically. Every day had one mission: grow the company. Now the mission was less clear. The money sat inside investment accounts, trusts, equity portfolios, and cash reserves far beyond anything Victor imagined as a young entrepreneur.

And strangely, the larger the fortune became, the more fragile it suddenly felt emotionally.

Victor started noticing something unsettling while attending private investor events and family office gatherings.

Many wealthy families were quietly losing fortunes.

Some lost wealth through taxes and poor planning. Others lost wealth through reckless spending. Some destroyed fortunes through lawsuits, divorces, family conflict, addiction, or failed succession planning.

Victor realized something deeply important.

Building wealth and protecting wealth required entirely different skill sets.

That realization changed the direction of his life completely.

Instead of immediately chasing new startups or luxury lifestyles, Victor became obsessed with studying long-term wealth preservation. He met privately with estate attorneys, tax strategists, family office executives, historians, behavioral psychologists, and multigenerational wealth advisors.

What he learned shocked him.

Most large fortunes disappear within three generations.

The pattern repeated constantly throughout history. One generation creates wealth through sacrifice and discipline. The second generation maintains some of it. The third generation often loses substantial portions due to lack of preparation, entitlement, poor governance, or emotional instability.

Victor refused to let that happen.

He began restructuring his entire approach to money.

First, he created multiple trusts designed to protect future appreciation and reduce estate tax exposure. Then he established a family office responsible for managing investments, legal coordination, risk oversight, and long-term planning.

But the most important decisions were not financial.

They were cultural.

Victor realized his future children might grow up without understanding struggle, discipline, or delayed gratification unless he intentionally created environments teaching those values.

So instead of building a life centered entirely around luxury, he focused on building a family culture centered around education, responsibility, curiosity, philanthropy, and entrepreneurship.

He funded educational programs for underserved students interested in cybersecurity. He created mentorship networks for young founders. He established charitable initiatives focused on digital safety and online privacy education.

For the first time since the acquisition, Victor felt meaningful purpose returning. Then an unexpected crisis arrived. A close friend named Daniel, another founder who sold a successful technology company years earlier, suffered catastrophic financial losses through reckless leveraged investments and speculative ventures. Within a relatively short period, Daniel lost hundreds of millions of dollars.

The situation deeply affected Victor emotionally.

Daniel was intelligent, ambitious, and highly successful—yet emotional overconfidence after sudden wealth destroyed much of his fortune.

Victor realized how dangerous unchecked ego could become after liquidity events.

From that moment forward, he approached wealth with far greater humility.

He diversified aggressively.

He avoided excessive leverage.

He focused on downside protection.

He developed long-term investment discipline instead of chasing constant excitement.

Most importantly, he stopped viewing wealth as a scoreboard. He began viewing it as responsibility. Years later, Victor's wealth continued growing steadily through disciplined investments, strong planning structures, and patient capital allocation. But what mattered most to him was not the number itself anymore.

It was the durability.

The sustainability.

The ability to create opportunities for future generations without destroying values in the process.

One evening during a private family dinner, Victor's teenage daughter asked him a question after overhearing a conversation about trusts and investments.

"Dad," she asked carefully, "why do you spend so much time protecting money when we already have enough?"

Victor smiled quietly before answering.

"Because real wealth isn't just about having money," he said. "It's about making sure opportunity survives long after you're gone."

She looked thoughtful for a moment.

Then Victor added the lesson that completely transformed his own understanding of success after the billion-dollar exit. "Anyone can spend wealth," he said softly. "The hard part is building systems strong enough to preserve wisdom along with the money."

Years later, that philosophy became the foundation not only of Victor's financial structures, but of the family legacy he ultimately left behind.

Chapter 9

Serial Entrepreneurship, Repeat Exits, and Building a Long-Term Founder Empire

Many people view entrepreneurship as a single-event journey. They imagine a founder building one company, achieving one major exit, and then retiring permanently into financial freedom. While this happens occasionally, some of the world's most influential entrepreneurs follow a very different path. Instead of stopping after one successful liquidity event, they use their experience, capital, networks, and credibility to build multiple companies, execute repeat exits, and create long-term entrepreneurial empires.

This is the mindset of the serial entrepreneur.

Serial entrepreneurship is not simply about starting multiple businesses randomly. It is about developing repeatable systems for identifying opportunities, building enterprise value, scaling strategically, leveraging capital, managing exits, and reinvesting wealth into increasingly larger ecosystems of ownership.

The first successful exit often changes everything.

Before the first major liquidity event, founders typically operate under severe constraints. Limited capital, uncertain credibility, restricted networks, operational pressure, and financial insecurity create enormous barriers. After a successful exit, however, founders gain resources that dramatically alter future opportunities.

Capital increases.

Credibility increases.

Relationships expand.

Investor access improves.

Media visibility grows.

Operational knowledge deepens.

Future fundraising becomes easier.

This creates entrepreneurial leverage.

Founders who successfully navigate one major company-building cycle often develop pattern recognition that allows them to move faster and more intelligently in future ventures. They understand hiring mistakes, fundraising dynamics, market timing, leadership development, operational systems, investor psychology, product-market fit, and exit preparation at much deeper levels.

Experience compounds.

This compounding effect is one reason many repeat founders create larger companies during later ventures than during their first businesses.

The first company often teaches survival.

The second teaches scale.

The third may teach empire building.

One of the most important psychological transformations after a successful exit involves the founder's relationship with fear.

During early entrepreneurial stages, fear often dominates decision-making. Founders worry about survival, personal finances, market failure, investor rejection, and operational collapse. These pressures can create emotional hesitation, defensive thinking, or excessive caution.

After successful liquidity events, however, many founders operate differently because survival fear decreases dramatically.

This creates strategic freedom. A founder no longer worried about paying basic living expenses may pursue larger opportunities, take longer-term risks, invest more aggressively in innovation, and think more expansively about market domination.

Ironically, reduced fear often improves entrepreneurial performance.

Another major advantage serial entrepreneurs possess is network leverage.

After successful exits, founders gain access to elite circles involving investors, executives, operators, institutional capital providers, media organizations, advisors, and strategic partners. Relationships that once seemed impossible suddenly become accessible.

This dramatically accelerates future ventures.

Top engineers become easier to recruit.

Investors respond faster.

Customers trust credibility more quickly.

Partnerships form more easily.

This network effect compounds over time. Sophisticated founders understand that relationships themselves become assets.

Another major shift involves capital allocation.

First-time founders often focus entirely on operating businesses. Serial entrepreneurs begin thinking like capital allocators. Instead of relying solely on personal labor or operational effort, they learn how to deploy capital strategically across multiple ventures, investments, acquisitions, partnerships, and ecosystems simultaneously.

This transition changes wealth creation dramatically.

Ownership diversification across multiple scalable businesses can create extraordinary long-term financial leverage.

For example, a founder who exits one technology company may later invest in dozens of startups, acquire complementary businesses, build holding companies, launch media brands, purchase real estate, fund venture studios, or create private investment firms.

Each successful venture strengthens the next.

This is how entrepreneurial ecosystems evolve into empires.

Another important concept is founder reputation.

In entrepreneurship, reputation compounds similarly to capital. Founders known for integrity, operational excellence, strategic intelligence, and successful exits often attract opportunities continuously.

Investors prefer backing proven operators.

Employees prefer joining respected leadership teams.

Acquisition opportunities emerge more frequently.

Media exposure increases naturally.

Reputation creates momentum.

This is why sophisticated entrepreneurs protect credibility aggressively.

One major difference between first-time founders and serial entrepreneurs is how they approach systems.

Inexperienced founders often build businesses reactively. Serial entrepreneurs intentionally build repeatable frameworks. They document hiring systems, operational structures, financial reporting processes, marketing playbooks, product development cycles, and leadership models that can be replicated across ventures.

This creates operational scalability beyond a single business. Some founders eventually operate portfolios of companies simultaneously because they understand how to install systems rather than personally controlling every operational detail.

This is a critical evolution.

Founders trapped inside daily operations often struggle to scale beyond one business. Founders who master systems can scale influence across multiple enterprises.

Another major advantage serial entrepreneurs gain involves fundraising efficiency.

After successful exits, institutional investors often proactively approach founders with funding opportunities. Investors understand that experienced operators possess lower execution risk compared to first-time founders.

This changes negotiation dynamics dramatically.

Instead of desperately seeking capital, experienced founders may choose strategically among multiple investors competing for access.

Leverage shifts.

Ownership preservation improves.

Terms become more favorable.

Sophisticated founders use this leverage carefully because they understand long-term wealth depends heavily on ownership structure. Another important characteristic of serial entrepreneurs is opportunity recognition.

Experienced founders often identify market shifts earlier because they understand how industries evolve. They recognize inefficiencies, behavioral changes, technological disruption, regulatory trends, and emerging demand patterns more quickly than less experienced operators.

Pattern recognition becomes a competitive advantage.

For example, founders who built internet businesses during early digital adoption later recognized opportunities in SaaS, cloud computing, AI, cybersecurity, fintech, digital media, creator economies, blockchain infrastructure, or automation earlier than broader markets.

This timing advantage can create enormous wealth.

Another important lesson serial entrepreneurs learn is the difference between building a company and building an ecosystem.

A company generates revenue through one primary business model.

An ecosystem creates interconnected value across multiple businesses, products, audiences, technologies, or industries.

Some of the world's wealthiest founders built ecosystems rather than isolated companies.

Technology platforms expanded into media.

Media brands expanded into software.

Software businesses expanded into financial services.

Consumer platforms expanded into infrastructure.

This interconnected growth creates compounding strategic leverage.

Each asset strengthens the others.

Another major shift occurs in risk management philosophy.

First-time founders often take concentrated operational risks because they lack alternatives. Serial entrepreneurs eventually balance aggressive innovation with portfolio-level risk management.

They may pursue high-risk startups while simultaneously owning stable cash-flow businesses, diversified investments, real estate assets, or venture portfolios.

This balance increases long-term durability.

Another important concept is acquisition strategy. Many serial entrepreneurs eventually shift from pure startup creation toward acquisition-based growth. Instead of building every business from scratch, they acquire undervalued companies, distressed assets, digital brands, operational businesses, or strategic technologies.

This accelerates scaling dramatically.

Experienced founders often recognize operational inefficiencies quickly and improve acquired businesses using systems developed through prior ventures.

This creates wealth multiplication.

Another critical lesson involves emotional evolution.

The first entrepreneurial journey often feels deeply personal. Founders attach emotionally to products, identities, and specific outcomes. Over time, sophisticated entrepreneurs develop greater emotional detachment from individual ventures.

This does not mean they care less.

It means they think more strategically.

They understand markets evolve constantly. Some ventures succeed enormously. Others fail despite strong execution. Emotional flexibility allows serial entrepreneurs to adapt rapidly without collapsing psychologically after setbacks.

Resilience compounds.

Another major factor in repeat founder success is talent attraction.

Elite employees often prefer working with experienced founders because prior success creates confidence. Strong leadership teams may follow successful founders across multiple ventures repeatedly.

This creates organizational momentum.

The quality of people surrounding a founder heavily influences future scalability.

Sophisticated founders therefore invest heavily in leadership development, culture, incentives, and long-term relationships.

Another critical transition involves moving from operator to architect.

Early-stage founders often personally manage nearly everything. Serial entrepreneurs increasingly focus on designing systems, recruiting leadership, allocating capital, and shaping long-term strategic direction rather than controlling every operational detail personally.

This creates scalability of influence. Some founders eventually oversee dozens of businesses indirectly through holding companies, venture studios, family offices, or investment groups.

Another important consideration is legacy.

After achieving financial freedom, many founders begin asking larger questions about impact, meaning, influence, and long-term contribution. Building multiple companies often becomes less about survival or money alone and more about solving meaningful problems, shaping industries, mentoring founders, supporting innovation, or creating lasting institutions.

This deeper motivation often fuels later entrepreneurial phases.

Another major lesson serial entrepreneurs learn is that exits themselves are not the ultimate goal.

Liquidity events create capital.

Capital creates optionality.

Optionality creates freedom.

Freedom allows founders to pursue larger visions.

This progression changes entrepreneurial psychology completely. Founders stop chasing money reactively and start designing long-term ecosystems intentionally. Another important factor involves intellectual property accumulation.

Serial entrepreneurs often build overlapping advantages across ventures including customer audiences, data infrastructure, media distribution, proprietary technology, operational frameworks, strategic partnerships, and investment networks.

This creates exponential leverage over time.

The founder is no longer building isolated businesses.

They are building interconnected strategic infrastructure.

Another major shift involves time horizons.

First-time entrepreneurs often think transactionally because survival dominates focus. Experienced founders think generationally. They build structures designed to compound over decades rather than optimize only short-term outcomes.

Compounding becomes the central philosophy.

Capital compounds.

Relationships compound.

Brand equity compounds.

Knowledge compounds.

Ownership compounds. Strategic positioning compounds.

This long-term orientation separates temporary success from enduring entrepreneurial empires.

Ultimately, serial entrepreneurship represents far more than repeatedly starting businesses.

It represents the evolution from founder to strategist.

From operator to architect.

From survival thinking to ecosystem thinking.

From single-company ownership to interconnected wealth creation.

The entrepreneurs who build lasting empires understand that one successful exit is not the end of the journey.

It is often only the beginning.

Because once a founder truly understands how ownership, systems, capital, networks, and liquidity interact together, entrepreneurship transforms from a career into a long-term engine of scalable influence and generational wealth creation.

And mastering that engine is how founders move beyond individual success toward building enduring entrepreneurial legacies.

The Founder Who Never Retired

When Ethan Cole sold his first software company at thirty-six years old, everyone expected him to disappear.

The acquisition made him wealthy enough to never work again. Financial media called the exit one of the most successful SaaS acquisitions of the year. Investors praised his operational discipline. Friends assumed he would spend the rest of his life traveling, relaxing, and enjoying the freedom most people only dream about.

At first, Ethan believed that too.

For nearly a decade, he had sacrificed almost everything to build the company. He missed vacations, relationships, birthdays, holidays, and countless personal moments while obsessively growing the business. The acquisition felt like the reward for surviving years of uncertainty and pressure.

During the first few months after the exit, Ethan embraced freedom completely.

He traveled through Europe.

He bought a modern home overlooking the ocean.

He played golf with investors and entrepreneurs who admired his success.

He invested passively in public markets and startup funds.

From the outside, his life looked perfect.

But privately, something unexpected happened.

He became restless.

Without the company, Ethan felt strangely disconnected from himself. For years, every day had structure, urgency, and meaning. Problems demanded solutions. Teams needed leadership. Markets created opportunities. Growth created momentum.

Now everything felt quiet.

Too quiet.

One evening during dinner with an older entrepreneur named Leonard Hayes, Ethan admitted his frustration openly.

"I thought financial freedom would feel different," Ethan said quietly.

Leonard smiled knowingly.

"That's because you think entrepreneurship was about money," he replied.

Ethan looked confused.

"What was it about then?"

Leonard leaned back in his chair calmly.

"Building."

That single word stayed in Ethan's mind for weeks.

Eventually, he realized Leonard was right.

The deepest satisfaction never came from bank accounts or headlines. It came from creating systems, solving problems, building teams, and shaping the future through ideas and execution.

Money was only the byproduct.

Once Ethan understood this, his entire perspective shifted.

Instead of retiring permanently, he started studying industries quietly again. He analyzed market inefficiencies, emerging technologies, and operational gaps. But this time, everything felt different because survival pressure no longer controlled him.

He could think bigger.

Longer term.

More strategically.

A year later, Ethan launched a small venture studio focused on AI automation businesses. Unlike his first startup, he approached this venture completely differently.

He built systems first.

He recruited elite operators early.

He structured ownership carefully.

He diversified across multiple products instead of relying on one company.

Most importantly, he used capital strategically instead of emotionally.

The results shocked even him.

Because he already understood hiring, fundraising, scaling, product development, investor psychology, and operational discipline, the new companies moved far faster than his first startup ever had.

Within four years, the venture studio controlled stakes in twelve rapidly growing businesses.

Some failed completely.

Several succeeded moderately. Two became extremely valuable.

Ethan discovered something powerful during this process.

The first company taught him survival.

The second phase taught him leverage.

For the first time, he realized entrepreneurship itself could become scalable.

Instead of personally operating one business forever, he could build ecosystems of companies connected through shared infrastructure, talent, distribution, and strategic partnerships.

That realization transformed his ambition completely.

Over the next decade, Ethan expanded aggressively into media, AI infrastructure, fintech platforms, digital education, and enterprise automation systems. Some companies were built internally. Others were acquired strategically.

Every new venture strengthened the broader ecosystem.

Media companies generated audiences.

Software companies monetized audiences.

AI infrastructure improved operational efficiency.

Education platforms trained future talent. Investment funds financed emerging startups.

The ecosystem began compounding.

At fifty years old, Ethan controlled a network of businesses far larger than the company that originally made him wealthy.

But more importantly, he finally understood something deeper about entrepreneurship.

True founder wealth was never only about one exit.

It was about building systems capable of creating opportunity repeatedly.

One afternoon, while mentoring a young founder preparing to sell his company, Ethan noticed the same emotional confusion he once felt years earlier.

The founder nervously asked him whether life would feel empty after the exit.

Ethan smiled slightly because he immediately recognized the fear behind the question.

"Only if you think the company is your identity," Ethan answered.

The founder looked uncertain.

Ethan continued.

"The exit doesn't end entrepreneurship. It changes your relationship with it."

Years later, during a private investor conference, someone asked Ethan why he kept building companies despite already having more money than he could ever spend.

He paused thoughtfully before answering.

"Because eventually you realize the real asset isn't the money," he said quietly. "It's the ability to create value repeatedly."

The audience remained silent.

Then Ethan added the lesson that defined his entire evolution from founder to empire builder.

"One successful company can make you wealthy. But learning how to build systems that repeatedly create wealth—that's when entrepreneurship becomes legacy."

Chapter 10

The Ultimate Founder Wealth Blueprint: Building Freedom, Influence, and Generational Opportunity Through Ownership

At the highest levels of entrepreneurship, wealth creation becomes far more than building a profitable business. It becomes the art of designing systems that generate long-term ownership, scalable value, strategic leverage, financial freedom, and enduring influence across generations. Founders who reach this level no longer think only about products, revenue, or even individual companies. They begin thinking in terms of ecosystems, capital allocation, ownership architecture, legacy, and compounding opportunity.

This is the ultimate founder wealth blueprint.

Everything explored throughout this book ultimately connects back to one central principle: ownership changes the trajectory of human life differently than income alone ever can.

Most people spend their lives operating within linear economic systems. They exchange time, labor, expertise, or attention for compensation. Their income depends largely on continued active participation. Founders who build scalable ownership structures, however, eventually operate within exponential systems. Enterprise value compounds. Equity appreciates. Capital generates additional opportunities. Networks expand. Strategic leverage multiplies.

This shift transforms entrepreneurship from a profession into a wealth-building framework.

The first stage of founder wealth creation usually begins with survival.

At this stage, entrepreneurs focus on basic execution. They search for product-market fit, acquire early customers, solve operational problems, generate revenue, and survive uncertainty. Most startups never move beyond this stage because entrepreneurship is emotionally and financially difficult. The majority of businesses fail before achieving meaningful scale.

Survival itself teaches valuable lessons.

Founders learn resilience, adaptability, discipline, sales psychology, customer behavior, operational problem-solving, and emotional endurance. They begin understanding that entrepreneurship is not about perfection. It is about persistence and continuous adaptation under uncertainty. The second stage involves scalability.

Once businesses achieve operational traction, founders begin building systems capable of expanding beyond personal labor limitations. This stage requires hiring, delegation, infrastructure development, recurring revenue systems, operational frameworks, technology leverage, and leadership evolution.

This is where founders transition from workers into builders of systems.

Many entrepreneurs become trapped because they never fully escape operator dependency. They build businesses that cannot function effectively without their constant involvement. These companies often generate income but struggle to create premium enterprisc value because scalability remains limited.

Sophisticated founders solve this by creating repeatable systems.

They document processes.

They build leadership teams.

They create infrastructure.

They automate operations.

They focus on scalability rather than simply activity.

This transition dramatically increases enterprise value because investors and buyers pay premium valuations for businesses capable of operating independently of one individual.

The third stage involves ownership leverage.

At this point, founders begin understanding that the real value of entrepreneurship often lies not in yearly income but in long-term equity appreciation. They recognize that scalable ownership can create wealth far beyond what salaries alone could ever produce.

This realization changes strategic thinking entirely.

Instead of maximizing short-term extraction, founders begin optimizing for enterprise growth, market positioning, recurring revenue, valuation expansion, intellectual property, network effects, and strategic leverage.

Ownership becomes the focus.

This stage often introduces institutional capital.

Venture capital firms, private equity groups, institutional investors, family offices, strategic acquirers, and public markets all become increasingly relevant. Sophisticated founders learn how to use external capital strategically without losing long-term vision or destroying ownership unnecessarily.

They understand dilution mathematically rather than emotionally.

They focus not only on ownership percentage but also on enterprise value growth.

This distinction separates small business thinking from large-scale wealth-building strategy.

The fourth stage involves liquidity.

Liquidity transforms paper wealth into usable financial power. IPOs, acquisitions, recapitalizations, secondary sales, and public market transactions create opportunities for founders to convert ownership into diversified assets, strategic freedom, and long-term capital allocation capability.

This stage is psychologically complex.

Many founders spend years chasing liquidity events without fully preparing emotionally for what happens afterward. Financial freedom removes survival pressure, but it also removes familiar structures that once defined identity and purpose.

Sophisticated founders prepare for this transition intentionally. They understand that money alone does not automatically create fulfillment, discipline, or direction. They develop long-term missions beyond individual exits.

This often leads to the fifth stage: capital allocation and ecosystem building.

At this level, founders stop thinking only as operators and begin thinking as architects of opportunity. They use capital strategically across investments, acquisitions, partnerships, media platforms, real estate, venture portfolios, private companies, and emerging technologies.

They create ecosystems.

Each asset strengthens the others.

A media company generates audience attention.

A software platform monetizes audience infrastructure.

A venture fund finances innovation.

An education platform develops talent.

A holding company acquires strategic assets.

An AI platform improves operational efficiency across the ecosystem. This interconnected leverage creates extraordinary compounding effects over time.

This is how entrepreneurial empires emerge.

Another major transformation at this stage involves time horizons.

Average market participants think short term.

Sophisticated founders think generationally.

They understand that the most powerful force in wealth creation is not sudden explosive success but sustained long-term compounding across decades.

Compounding affects everything.

Capital compounds.

Relationships compound.

Reputation compounds.

Knowledge compounds.

Brand equity compounds.

Ownership compounds.

Strategic positioning compounds. The founders who understand this stop chasing short-term appearances and begin designing systems intended to survive and expand over long periods.

This long-term orientation creates enormous advantages.

Another important element of the ultimate founder wealth blueprint is optionality.

Optionality means maintaining flexibility to pursue multiple future opportunities rather than becoming trapped within rigid structures. Sophisticated founders preserve optionality intentionally through diversified ownership, strategic liquidity, operational scalability, financial discipline, and network development.

Optionality creates resilience.

When industries shift, optionality allows adaptation.

When new technologies emerge, optionality creates opportunity.

When markets collapse temporarily, optionality preserves stability.

This is why preserving flexibility becomes so important after wealth is created.

Another major lesson sophisticated founders eventually learn is that reputation may become more valuable than capital itself.

Money opens doors initially.

Reputation determines which doors remain open long term.

Founders known for integrity, operational excellence, strategic intelligence, ethical leadership, and long-term value creation attract opportunities continuously. Investors trust them. Employees follow them. Institutions support them. Partnerships form naturally.

Reputation compounds similarly to ownership.

This is why sophisticated entrepreneurs protect credibility aggressively.

Another critical aspect of founder wealth involves leadership evolution.

Every stage of growth requires different leadership abilities.

The founder capable of launching a startup may not automatically possess the skills required to lead a public company, manage institutional capital, oversee multiple businesses, or preserve generational wealth.

Sophisticated founders evolve continuously.

They become better communicators. Better decision-makers. Better capital allocators. Better strategic thinkers.

Better emotional managers.

This internal evolution often determines long-term success more than external market conditions alone.

Another important realization involves emotional discipline.

Markets fluctuate.

Valuations rise and fall.

Public sentiment changes rapidly.

Economic cycles create volatility.

Founders who tie emotional identity directly to short-term outcomes often experience burnout, impulsiveness, or instability.

Sophisticated founders learn emotional detachment from temporary market noise.

They focus on systems, execution, long-term value creation, and strategic positioning rather than obsessing over daily fluctuations.

This emotional maturity becomes increasingly important as wealth grows because larger decisions create larger consequences.

Another essential component of long-term founder wealth is team building.

No meaningful empire is built alone.

The strongest founders learn how to identify talent, align incentives, build culture, delegate authority, and create leadership structures capable of scaling independently.

This is one of the most difficult entrepreneurial transitions because many founders initially believe they must control everything personally.

Eventually, they realize true scale requires trust and organizational leverage.

Leadership becomes multiplication.

Another critical factor involves innovation.

The business world evolves continuously. Founders who stop adapting eventually lose relevance regardless of prior success. Sophisticated entrepreneurs remain intellectually curious. They study emerging technologies, behavioral trends, macroeconomic shifts, regulatory developments, and changing consumer psychology constantly.

Curiosity protects longevity.

The founders who survive across decades are often not those who begin strongest, but those who continue learning the longest.

Another major component of the ultimate wealth blueprint is mission.

Money alone rarely sustains long-term motivation after basic financial security is achieved. Many founders eventually realize that fulfillment comes from contribution, impact, creativity, innovation, mentorship, philanthropy, or solving meaningful problems.

This deeper purpose fuels later entrepreneurial stages.

Some founders fund scientific research.

Others support education.

Some invest in future technologies.

Others mentor emerging entrepreneurs or build institutions designed to improve society over generations.

At the highest levels, entrepreneurship often evolves into stewardship. Another major realization sophisticated founders eventually have is that ownership creates influence beyond personal wealth. Capital shapes industries. Innovation shapes culture. Technology shapes society. Media shapes perception.

Education shapes future generations.

Founders controlling scalable systems often influence far more than financial outcomes alone.

This is why ethical responsibility becomes increasingly important as influence expands.

The strongest founders recognize that long-term success requires balancing ambition with integrity.

Another essential lesson is that failure never disappears entirely.

Even experienced founders encounter setbacks, market collapses, failed investments, operational crises, leadership mistakes, and unexpected disruption. What changes is resilience.

Sophisticated founders recover faster because they understand cycles.

They remain adaptable.

They preserve optionality.

They avoid emotional collapse during volatility.

Resilience compounds similarly to capital.

Ultimately, the ultimate founder wealth blueprint is not about becoming rich quickly.

It is about designing systems capable of generating scalable opportunity repeatedly over long periods.

It is about understanding ownership.

Understanding leverage.

Understanding capital.

Understanding markets.

Understanding psychology.

Understanding leadership.

Understanding compounding.

And most importantly, understanding that entrepreneurship at its highest level is not merely about making money.

It is about building value so durable, scalable, and meaningful that it continues creating opportunity long after the founder's original effort began.

That is the real power of ownership.

That is the true meaning of founder wealth creation.

And that is how entrepreneurs transform ideas into freedom, influence, generational opportunity, and lasting legacy.

The Last Meeting Before the Legacy Began

At sixty-three years old, Marcus Holloway no longer cared much about headlines.

Earlier in life, headlines mattered deeply.

When he launched his first software company at twenty-seven, he obsessed over recognition constantly. Every investor article, valuation increase, conference invitation, and media mention felt emotionally important. Success felt tied to visibility.

Now, decades later, Marcus viewed success differently.

He sat quietly inside the conference room overlooking downtown Miami while his legal team prepared the final documents for the restructuring of his family holding company. Outside the windows, sunlight reflected across the skyline while ships moved slowly through the harbor below.

The meeting itself looked ordinary.

But Marcus understood its significance completely.

This was not just another business transaction. It was the beginning of his family's long-term legacy structure.

The journey to that moment had taken nearly forty years.

Marcus built his first company during the early days of enterprise software expansion. The business started modestly from a rented office with outdated computers and unpaid interns working long nights fueled by caffeine and ambition.

For years, survival consumed him completely.

He maxed out credit cards.

He slept in the office occasionally.

He pitched investors endlessly.

He lost relationships.

He doubted himself constantly.

But eventually the company scaled successfully. An acquisition followed years later, creating life-changing wealth far beyond anything Marcus imagined as a struggling young founder.

At first, he thought the money itself was the finish line.

It wasn't.

After the acquisition, Marcus launched another company.

Then another. Then a private investment group.

Then a media platform.

Then a cybersecurity infrastructure fund.

Over decades, the businesses expanded into a network of interconnected companies generating enormous enterprise value collectively.

At some point, Marcus stopped thinking like a founder of individual businesses.

He started thinking like an architect of systems.

That transformation changed everything.

His wealth no longer depended on one company. It flowed through diversified ownership structures, operating businesses, investments, intellectual property, real estate, media infrastructure, and strategic partnerships spanning multiple industries.

The ecosystem itself became the asset.

Yet despite enormous financial success, Marcus carried one persistent fear quietly for years:

Would everything collapse after he was gone? He had watched too many wealthy families self-destruct across generations. Some lost fortunes through lawsuits, addiction, entitlement, reckless investing, family conflict, or poor succession planning.

Marcus refused to let that happen.

So instead of focusing only on preserving money, he focused on preserving philosophy.

He spent years teaching his children about ownership, investing, entrepreneurship, emotional discipline, and responsibility. They attended business meetings growing up. They studied financial statements. They volunteered through family philanthropic foundations.

Marcus wanted them to understand something deeper than wealth itself.

He wanted them to understand stewardship.

That was why this meeting mattered so much.

The new holding structure would eventually transfer ownership gradually across future generations while preserving operational governance standards, educational requirements, philanthropic commitments, and long-term capital allocation principles.

Marcus was not simply protecting money.

He was protecting culture.

One of his attorneys finally slid the final documents across the table.

Marcus signed slowly.

As the pen lifted from the paper, he felt unexpectedly emotional.

Not because of the numbers involved.

But because he realized something important.

The companies themselves were never the real legacy.

The real legacy was the systems capable of creating opportunity repeatedly long after his own lifetime ended.

Later that evening, Marcus walked alone through one of the campuses operated by his education foundation. Students filled the hallways discussing technology, entrepreneurship, engineering, and artificial intelligence.

Many came from backgrounds similar to his own decades earlier.

Limited resources.

Big ambition.

No clear roadmap.

As Marcus watched them, he understood the full meaning of founder wealth for the first time.

Wealth was never only about accumulation.

Real wealth meant creating systems that expanded opportunity for others.

A young student eventually recognized him and nervously approached.

"Mr. Holloway," the student asked carefully, "what was the most important thing you learned after building all those companies?"

Marcus smiled quietly.

There were thousands of possible answers.

But only one felt true enough.

"The goal was never the companies," he said softly.

The student looked confused.

Marcus continued.

"The companies were just vehicles."

"For what?" the student asked.

Marcus looked out across the campus thoughtfully before answering.

"For building freedom," he said. "Freedom to create. Freedom to think long term. Freedom to help others build something bigger than themselves."

The student nodded slowly.

Then Marcus added the lesson that defined his entire life journey from struggling founder to legacy architect.

"Money can change your lifestyle," he said quietly. "But ownership, discipline, and vision—that's what changes generations."

Final IPO Thoughts

The journey from founder to wealth creator is one of the most transformative experiences in modern business. It is a path filled with uncertainty, ambition, sacrifice, reinvention, pressure, opportunity, emotional growth, and strategic evolution. Throughout this book, we explored one of the most important realities of entrepreneurship: wealth is not created only through hard work alone. It is created through ownership, scalability, strategic positioning, liquidity planning, and the intelligent use of capital markets.

This distinction changes everything.

Most people spend their lives focused on income. Founders who create extraordinary wealth eventually learn to focus on equity, enterprise value, systems, and ownership leverage. They understand that scalable ownership can generate financial outcomes far beyond what linear labor alone could ever produce. This is the central principle behind modern founder wealth creation.

The world's largest entrepreneurial fortunes were rarely built through salaries.

They were built through ownership in scalable enterprises.

This is why understanding IPOs, equity structures, liquidity events, institutional capital, dilution strategy, public markets, and wealth preservation is so important. These are not simply financial concepts reserved for billionaires or Wall Street professionals. They are the mechanics behind how modern wealth compounds.

Every major company begins with an idea.

But ideas alone are never enough.

The founders who ultimately create lasting wealth are the ones who learn how to transform ideas into systems. They build products that solve real problems. They develop operational discipline. They attract talent. They create recurring revenue. They establish strategic positioning. They learn how investors think. They understand scalability. They adapt continuously as markets evolve.

Most importantly, they understand that enterprise value itself becomes an asset.

This is one of the greatest mindset shifts in entrepreneurship.

A founder stops thinking only about making money today and begins thinking about building something valuable enough to appreciate over decades. This long-term perspective changes decision-making dramatically. Every hire, every customer, every system, every operational improvement, every strategic partnership, and every innovation becomes part of a much larger wealth-building process.

The companies that eventually attract institutional investors, acquisitions, or public market attention are rarely accidental successes.

They are engineered intentionally.

Founders who build enterprise value intelligently focus on durability, scalability, operational excellence, leadership quality, financial structure, market opportunity, and long-term positioning. They understand that sophisticated investors and buyers evaluate companies differently than average consumers do. Investors seek predictability, leverage, growth potential, defensibility, and strategic importance.

This is why understanding capital markets matters.

Capital markets are not separate from entrepreneurship.

They are extensions of entrepreneurship.

Public markets, venture capital, private equity, institutional investment, secondary transactions, acquisitions, recapitalizations, and IPOs all represent different mechanisms through which ownership becomes scalable financial opportunity.

Founders who understand these systems gain tremendous leverage.

Throughout this book, we explored how dilution can either weaken or multiply founder wealth depending on how it is managed. We explored how strategic fundraising can accelerate growth dramatically while also creating risks surrounding control and ownership structure. We explored how liquidity events transform paper wealth into usable capital, and how sophisticated founders think carefully about timing, taxes, diversification, and long-term preservation.

One of the most important lessons in entrepreneurship is that creating wealth and preserving wealth are not the same thing.

Many founders spend years learning how to scale businesses but never learn how to protect wealth afterward. This is why taxes, trusts, estate planning, diversification, family governance, philanthropy, and long-term investment strategy become increasingly important after major liquidity events occur.

The founder journey eventually evolves beyond simple financial accumulation.

At the beginning, survival dominates thinking.

Then growth dominates thinking.

Then scale dominates thinking.

Eventually, legacy begins to dominate thinking.

Sophisticated founders eventually realize that true wealth is not only measured by personal lifestyle. It is measured by durability, impact, freedom, opportunity creation, and the ability to build systems that continue generating value beyond one lifetime.

This is where entrepreneurship becomes legacy building.

One of the most fascinating realities about IPOs and public markets is that they often represent both an ending and a beginning simultaneously.

For years, founders work privately, building quietly through uncertainty and risk. The IPO may appear to outsiders as the final reward for success. Yet in reality, becoming a public company introduces entirely new responsibilities, pressures, expectations, and psychological challenges.

Public company leadership requires emotional resilience.

Public markets fluctuate constantly. Analysts react to earnings reports. Investors shift sentiment rapidly. Media narratives change daily. Founders who tie personal emotional stability directly to stock prices often struggle psychologically after IPOs.

The strongest public founders learn to focus on long-term enterprise value rather than short-term market volatility.

They understand that public markets are emotional in the short term but often rational over the long term. They remain focused on execution, innovation, leadership, and sustainable growth rather than reacting emotionally to daily fluctuations.

This emotional discipline becomes one of the greatest competitive advantages in public company leadership.

Another major lesson throughout this book is the importance of adaptability.

Markets evolve continuously.

Technology changes rapidly.

Consumer behavior shifts.

Regulations transform industries.

Economic cycles fluctuate.

Founders who survive and thrive over decades are rarely the ones who resist change. They are the ones who adapt strategically while preserving core vision and operational integrity.

Adaptability compounds.

So does experience.

This is why serial entrepreneurs often create larger and more durable wealth during later ventures. They learn pattern recognition. They understand capital allocation. They build stronger networks. They develop emotional resilience. They move from operator thinking toward architect thinking.

Eventually, entrepreneurship itself becomes scalable.

Some founders stop building single businesses and begin building ecosystems of ownership, influence, and strategic leverage across multiple industries, technologies, and markets.

This is where entrepreneurship evolves into empire building.

One of the deepest truths about founder wealth creation is that ownership creates freedom differently than income ever can.

Income may support lifestyle.

Ownership creates leverage. Ownership allows wealth to appreciate while systems continue operating beyond direct labor input. Ownership creates optionality, flexibility, and long-term strategic freedom.

This is why equity matters so much.

Founders who understand ownership structures, liquidity planning, capital markets, and enterprise scalability position themselves very differently than those focused only on short-term income generation.

They begin building assets rather than simply creating jobs for themselves.

This distinction often determines whether entrepreneurs remain financially dependent on active labor forever or eventually achieve true long-term financial independence.

Another important lesson is that entrepreneurship is deeply psychological.

The external business strategies matter enormously, but internal emotional management matters equally. Fear, ego, insecurity, greed, impatience, identity attachment, comparison, pressure, and emotional reactivity can all destroy founder wealth if left unmanaged.

Many founders fail not because of intelligence deficits, but because of emotional instability during periods of pressure, growth, success, or volatility. This is why emotional maturity becomes increasingly important as wealth grows.

Money amplifies psychology.

Public visibility amplifies psychology.

Leadership amplifies psychology.

Founders who develop self-awareness, discipline, resilience, patience, and long-term thinking often preserve wealth and influence more effectively than those driven entirely by emotional impulses.

This is especially true after liquidity events occur.

Many founders discover that financial freedom alone does not automatically create fulfillment. Some feel lost after exits because they spent years attaching identity entirely to company growth. Others struggle with purpose after survival pressure disappears.

This is why mission matters.

The strongest founders eventually build not only for money but also for meaning, impact, innovation, and long-term contribution.

That deeper motivation often sustains long-term entrepreneurial evolution.

Another important truth is that opportunity rarely arrives in perfect form.

Most successful founders begin with uncertainty, rejection, limited resources, and imperfect circumstances. Very few entrepreneurs feel fully prepared at the beginning. Confidence often develops through action rather than before action.

This is why execution matters so much.

Ideas are common.

Execution is rare.

Consistency is rare.

Resilience is rare.

Long-term discipline is rare.

The entrepreneurs who create extraordinary outcomes are often not the smartest people in the room initially. They are the people who continue learning, adapting, building, and executing over long periods while others quit.

Persistence compounds.

So does ownership. Throughout this book, one central theme remained consistent: wealth creation through entrepreneurship is ultimately about building value.

Not hype.

Not appearances.

Not temporary attention.

Real value.

Businesses that solve meaningful problems, create leverage, improve systems, strengthen industries, increase efficiency, build trust, or create scalable infrastructure often become enormously valuable because value itself attracts capital.

Investors chase value.

Markets reward value.

Customers remain loyal to value.

Public markets eventually recognize sustainable value.

This is why operational excellence always matters more than temporary excitement over long periods.

Founders who focus obsessively on creating real value place themselves in position to benefit from future liquidity events, acquisitions, institutional investment, and public market opportunities naturally.

Another important lesson is that long-term thinking creates disproportionate advantages.

Most people think in weeks or months.

Many businesses think in quarters.

Sophisticated founders think in decades.

This long-term orientation affects every decision.

Hiring decisions improve.

Brand building improves.

Operational systems improve.

Capital allocation improves.

Reputation compounds.

Relationships strengthen.

Strategic patience creates leverage.

Founders who think long term often appear slower initially but build far stronger foundations over time.

And strong foundations create durable wealth. One of the most powerful realizations any entrepreneur can have is understanding that capital itself can become scalable once enough ownership leverage exists.

At first, founders trade labor for survival.

Then they build systems.

Then systems create cash flow.

Then cash flow creates enterprise value.

Then enterprise value creates liquidity.

Then liquidity creates investment capacity.

Then capital begins generating additional opportunities independently.

This progression transforms the founder from worker into owner, from owner into investor, and eventually from investor into allocator of influence and opportunity.

That transformation is the true power of entrepreneurship.

Ultimately, IPOs and major liquidity events are not only financial milestones.

They are reflections of value creation at scale. They represent years of sacrifice, adaptation, execution, leadership, and vision finally converging into public recognition and financial leverage.

But the greatest founders understand that the IPO itself is never the ultimate destination.

It is simply one chapter in a much larger journey.

A journey involving ownership.

A journey involving growth.

A journey involving strategic freedom.

A journey involving legacy.

The founders who build lasting wealth are not merely chasing money.

They are building systems capable of creating value repeatedly across time, industries, generations, and markets.

And once a founder truly understands how ownership, enterprise value, capital markets, liquidity strategy, and long-term thinking work together, entrepreneurship transforms from uncertain survival into one of the most powerful wealth-building vehicles ever created.

That is the true lesson behind IPOs, founder equity, and capital markets.

Not simply how companies go public.

But how vision, ownership, discipline, and strategic execution can transform ideas into lasting financial freedom, scalable influence, and generational opportunity.

www.ingramcontent.com/pod-product-compliance
Lightning Source LLC
LaVergne TN
LVHW040517210926
848480LV00007BA/1497
9798256015787